A first in Indian financial publishing

Investing in India's Compounding Decade

STRATEGIC WEALTH CREATION FOR DOCTORS

Tejaswi Sanga

Foreword by Dr. A.V. Gurava Reddy

notionpress.com

INDIA • SINGAPORE • MALAYSIA

Paperback ISBN: 979-8-90560-353-2
Hardcase ISBN: 979-8-90560-354-9

To every Indian doctor who gave the best years of their life to medicine.

May this book give something back.

CONTENTS

What Doctors are Saying

"A comprehensive and well-crafted guide to investment planning for medical professionals. The book lays out a clear path to building steady wealth — ensuring that your hard-earned money works as hard as you do. For NRI doctors like me returning to India, it serves as an especially valuable ready reckoner to the investment avenues available in this country. Congratulations to Tejaswi for bringing together every important aspect of financial management in one place."

— Dr. Venkat S. Munukutla
Pain Physician & Anesthesiologist

"Strategic Wealth Creation for Doctors is a must-read for young doctors. It offers practical guidance on financial planning, wealth building, and securing one's future from the very start of a medical career. A highly relevant and valuable book for every doctor starting out."

— Dr. Chandramouli S. Mantravadi
Cardiologist & Electrophysiologist

"It is a pleasure to come across a book so well written, offering a step-by-step approach to investment planning for doctors who have little time and even less knowledge of personal finance. It deeply understands the apprehensions doctors carry around investments and addresses them with clarity and purpose. A must-read for every doctor who wants to become a more informed and confident investor."

— Dr. Roshan Kumar Jaiswal
Pediatric Orthopedic Surgeon

"A much-needed and practical guide that every doctor should read early in their career. Tejaswi simplifies complex financial concepts and presents them in a way that is both relevant and actionable for medical professionals. This is the kind of knowledge we never receive during our training — honestly, I wish every doctor read a book like this alongside their MBBS. A valuable resource for building financial clarity and long-term security."

— Dr. (Maj.) Harikrishnan Vannadil
Ophthalmology Surgeon

"Strategic Wealth Creation for Doctors is a highly relevant and much-needed financial guide for the medical fraternity. Doctors dedicate their lives to patient care, often with little exposure to financial literacy, wealth management, taxation, or retirement planning — this book thoughtfully addresses every one of those gaps. The chapter flow reflects a deep understanding of a doctor's financial journey, from income management and risk protection to wealth accumulation, succession, and legacy creation. Presented not merely as theory, but as actionable guidance at every stage of a medical career, it is a valuable financial companion for every doctor striving to build discipline, independence, and long-term security alongside their noble profession."

— Dr. P. V. Saiprasada Rao
Senior Paediatrician

"This book, arguably the first of its kind for doctors in India, stands alongside — and in many ways surpasses — its well-known American counterpart, The White Coat Investor, in its understanding of how doctors relate to money across different life phases and risk profiles. For NRI doctors, it is a comprehensive gateway guide to investing in India, combining depth with brevity in equal measure. A must for every doctor's personal library."

— Dr. Anita Pasumarthy
Nephrologist

"Strategic Wealth Creation for Doctors is a thoughtful and comprehensive financial guide that captures the unique realities of a doctor's life — long working hours, a delayed earning phase, limited financial literacy, lifestyle inflation, peer pressure, and an overdependence on real estate. Tejaswi Sanga combines practical financial wisdom with deep insight into the psychology and career journey of a doctor. Written in a simple, structured, and relatable manner, it is a valuable guide for every doctor aspiring to achieve long-term financial security and independence."

— Dr. Narayanam Srinivas
Senior Consultant Urologist

"As a Senior Dermatologist and Cosmetic Laser Specialist, I only wish a book like this had been available at the start of my career. Strategic Wealth Creation for Doctors is lucid, concise, and a genuine eye-opener. I wish I had known these principles — XIRR, liquidity planning, retirement strategy — much earlier in my financial life. For doctor couples like

my wife and me, this book offers a practical framework to plan your wealth creation journey together, in harmony. A must-read for every doctor."

— Dr. K.S. Ram

Senior Dermatologist & Cosmetic Laser Specialist

FOREWORD

"It is a wonderful read — Tejaswi's book on *Strategic Wealth Creation for Doctors* spans an extensive 40 chapters. Interestingly, he has discussed the psychology of doctors and the financial blind spots of the medical community, which I completely understand because I am one of them. It is a general consensus that doctors are excellent human beings and good clinicians, but poor financial planners — with some exceptions like my good old friend, Dr. Bharat Modi from Gujarat.

It is a very compelling read for all doctors. The beauty is that each chapter is written in precise and simple language — even the most time-pressed doctor can read it and understand. Another important feature is the case studies, which compare different scenarios across doctors at different career stages and sub-specialties. Creating wealth for hardworking doctors is definitely an important topic, and I am sure every doctor will appreciate this — especially given the long incubation period before a doctor enters the earning range.

Doctors value precision, and this book delivers exactly that. It will give every doctor a head start — right from the early days of their career. I hope Tejaswi goes on to write many more such books and continues to create value for the medical community."

Dr. A.V. Gurava Reddy
Managing Director & Chief Joint Replacement Surgeon
KIMS-Sunshine Hospitals

PREFACE

As a child, I wanted to be a doctor. That dream did not materialise — but the fascination never left. Over the years, as my career took me deep into financial markets, banking, and personal finance, I found myself drawn, repeatedly and almost inevitably, towards the medical profession. Not as a patient, but as an observer. And what I observed, over hundreds of conversations across more than two decades, gradually unsettled me.

I had assumed — as many do — that doctors, by virtue of their education and earnings, were financially sophisticated. The conversations told a different story. Doctors, I discovered, are among the most financially underserved professionals in India. Not because they lack intelligence or discipline — they possess both in abundance — but because no structured, honest, India-specific resource exists for them. In its absence, the vacuum has been filled by bank relationship managers chasing commission targets, by social media myths that spread faster than they can be verified, and by well-meaning but misaligned advice that treats a doctor's income as an opportunity rather than a responsibility.

That realisation carried a quiet anger with it. Doctors spend the prime years of their lives — years that most professionals use to build financial foundations — in training, in residency, in the long and uncompensated apprenticeship that medicine demands. By the time income finally arrives, the habits of financial neglect are already formed, the myths already believed, the wrong products already purchased. People who dedicate their lives to the health of others deserve far better than being taken for granted because they are too busy, or too trusting, to question what they are being sold.

This book is my attempt to address that gap. It is not a theoretical text on personal finance. It is a structured, practical framework built entirely around the financial realities of Indian doctors — the late start, the compressed earning window, the cash flow pressures of private practice, the illiquidity of real estate-heavy portfolios, the behavioural traps that a demanding profession creates. Each chapter is written to be read in the time between consultations, not in a weekend retreat. Each case study is drawn from real financial journeys — real choices, real consequences, real recoveries.

The timing of this book is not coincidental. India is in the midst of a compounding decade — a convergence of demographic energy, deepening capital markets, expanding investment infrastructure, and economic momentum that creates a generational opportunity for wealth creation. Indian doctors, many of whom are entering or approaching their peak earning years precisely as this window opens, are uniquely positioned to benefit from it. But this window will not stay open indefinitely, and it rewards only those who are structured to receive what it offers. That urgency runs through every chapter of this book.

My hope is that you read this with an open mind. If some of what you find here reflects decisions you have already made — decisions that, in retrospect, you wish had gone differently — do not feel unsettled. Every pattern described in this book is reversible if caught early enough, and manageable even if caught late. The frameworks here are not judgements. They are tools. Put them to work.

Question every financial decision rationally. Do not lose sight of the process in the hope that outcomes will take care of themselves. Set your goals with the same precision you bring to a diagnosis. And remember — *you do not plan to fail. You only fail to plan.*

The financial life you want is entirely within reach. This book shows you how to structure it. The rest depends on you. Plan the trade. Then trade the plan.

Tejaswi Sanga
Hyderabad

Acknowledgements

This book carries a foreword by **Dr. A.V. Gurava Reddy**, Managing Director and Chief Joint Replacement Surgeon at KIMS-Sunshine Hospitals — and I am deeply grateful for far more than his name on the cover. Despite a schedule that would exhaust most people, he read this book in its entirety, word by word. His perspective as a doctor-entrepreneur — someone who has lived the four decades of a doctor's professional life with uncommon intention — gave this book an insider clarity that no amount of external research could have provided. His words did not merely endorse the book. They directed it.

Dr. Krishna Subramaniam shaped this book in a way that is both professional and personal. As my surgeon, he reconstructed my ligaments. As a reviewer, he helped me understand the particular financial fragility of a corporate doctor's career — a perspective that sharpened several chapters considerably. His insightful questions challenged me to clarify concepts I had assumed were self-evident. I am indebted to him on both counts.

Dr. Chandramouli Mantravadi and **Dr. Roshan Kumar Jaiswal** brought thoughtful nuance to the drafts — not merely trimming what was excessive, but helping expand what was incomplete. Their engagement pushed the scope of this book well beyond where it might otherwise have stopped.

Shri Harkara Srinivasa Rao, for his steadfast encouragement across my years in financial markets and for opening doors that shaped the credibility of this work. Some contributions are invisible to the reader but foundational to the book — his is one of them.

My wife **Bhavya** is my first reader and my most honest critic. She does not mince words, and this book is better for it. Without her — and without the cooperation and patience of my two sons, **Pradyumna** and **Parjanya** — I could not have seen this through. My **parents**, who have always trusted and blessed every writing endeavour I have undertaken, remain the quiet foundation beneath everything I do.

My brother **Chaitanya** and my friend **Vijay Bhaskar** gave generously of their time — across critical reviews and the painstaking work of formatting — despite long working hours of their own. The book has taken its final shape in no small part because of their patience and effort.

Finally, to the scores of doctors who trusted me with their finances over the years — who asked difficult questions, shared their anxieties, and allowed me into their financial lives at moments of both confidence and uncertainty — this book belongs as much to you as it does to me. Your journeys provided the behavioural insights that no textbook could have offered. I hope this book returns some of that value.

Chapter 1

Why Doctors Must Think About Money Differently

1.1 — The Paradox of the Indian Doctor

Few professions in India command the respect, trust, and gratitude that medicine does. Yet Indian doctors often struggle with wealth creation — not due to lack of intelligence or earning ability, but because the medical career path is fundamentally misaligned with wealth-building timelines.

Doctors mature professionally over time. Wealth rewards early financial maturity. Most doctors recognise this mismatch only after 40, when years of hard work lead to an unsettling question:

> ***"I have worked relentlessly for over a decade — why doesn't my net worth reflect it?"***

This book answers that — through a framework built specifically for medical careers.

1.2 — A Doctor's Earning Curve Starts Late

A typical doctor's earning timeline:

- Age 18–23: MBBS
- Age 23–26: Internship & PG preparation
- Age 26–30: MD / MS / DNB
- Age 30–34: Super-specialisation (for many)
- Age 32–35: Stable earning finally begins

By then, peers in engineering, management, or IT have had a full decade of earnings, savings, and compounding already working. That gap is not recoverable through higher income alone.

Two professionals. Same ₹50,000 monthly investment at 14% annual return. One starts at age 23. The other — a doctor — starts at age 33.

Corpus at age 60, starting at 23: **~₹74 crore**

Corpus at age 60, starting at 33: **~₹18 crore**

Gap from ten lost years: **~₹56 crore**

No product, no strategy, and no level of income can manufacture those ten missing years of compounding. This is the single most consequential financial reality of a doctor's life.

Compounding is like residency — start late, and the later years are harder.

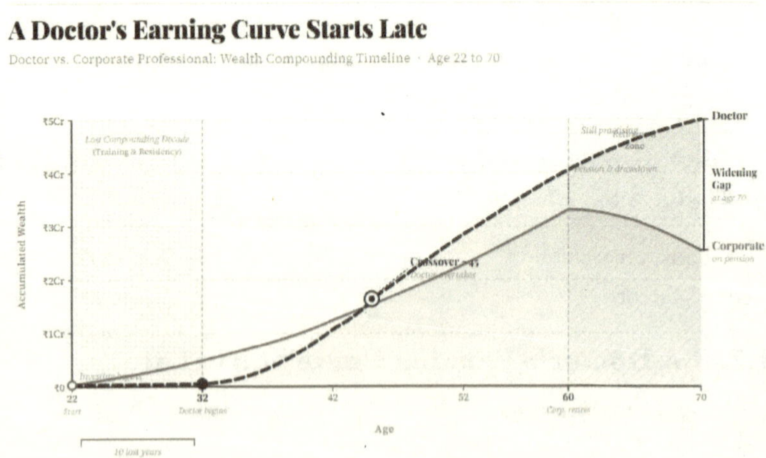

Figure 1.2 — The compounding gap between a doctor and a corporate professional who started investing ten years earlier.

1.3 — The Prestige Trap: When Respect ≠ Wealth

Respect does not compound — investments do.

Respect comes early. Wealth comes late. This gap creates pressure to look successful long before real financial security is built — bigger cars, larger homes, premium clinics, and constant comparison with peers.

"Society expects us to live like millionaires long before we actually become one."

Prestige-driven spending does not merely reduce savings. It diverts capital away from compounding during the exact years when compounding would have had the greatest impact.

1.4 — The Doctor, The Corporate, and The Investor

Every day, doctors are at the centre of one of India's fastest-growing industries. Hospital stocks grow. Pharmaceutical companies compound. Diagnostics platforms scale.

You prescribe the medicines. The manufacturers earn the returns. You admit the patients. The hospital stocks grow.

Here is an uncomfortable but important question: **Are you participating in the wealth you help create every day?**

India's capital markets now give every doctor a seat at the table of the very industry they serve. Whether that seat is taken is entirely a matter of intention and structure.

1.5 — Why Doctors Need a Tailored Financial Playbook

Generic financial advice fails doctors because it ignores six realities specific to the profession:

1. **Unpredictable income** — revenues and payouts fluctuate with seasons, hospitals, and TPAs
2. **High professional risk** — litigation and complications are occupational realities

3. **Fixed liabilities, variable cash flows** — EMIs don't pause during lean periods
4. **Late savings, early responsibilities** — many doctors work into their late sixties out of necessity
5. **Overexposure to real estate** — poor liquidity and weak real returns
6. **Constant social pressure** — family expectations and peer comparison distort decisions

> A plan built for a salaried professional will not serve a doctor well. **The biggest risk is not a wrong investment — it is a framework that was never designed for your life.**

1.6 — Indian Doctors at a Unique Financial Intersection

Indian doctors today sit at a rare convergence of opportunity:

- India is among the world's fastest-growing major economies — projected to become the third-largest by the early 2030s
- Per-capita income is crossing thresholds that historically trigger rapid expansion in financial markets
- Healthcare demand is rising structurally — driven by demographics, chronic disease, and rising insurance penetration
- Capital markets are deeper, better-regulated, and more accessible than at any previous point in India's history
- New structures — PMS, AIFs, REITs, InvITs, SIFs, GIFT City platforms — offer access to asset classes unavailable a decade ago

This is India's compounding decade. Doctors who build the right financial structure now will compound alongside the country's growth. Those who delay will watch that window narrow.

> **Favourable conditions are not enough.** Wealth compounds only when investing is intentional, structured, and life-stage aligned. That alignment is what this book is designed to create.

1.7 — The Purpose of This Book

This is not a theory book or a product pitch. It is a practical playbook — built around the specific realities of a medical career — to help doctors:

- Diagnose their financial blind spots early
- Allocate capital correctly across life stages
- Avoid unsuitable products and structural mistakes that quietly cost more than any market correction
- Build a portfolio that compounds steadily — without requiring daily attention or financial expertise

You will learn how major asset classes actually work, how to manage liquidity and volatility, and how to design retirement income you control.

Most importantly, you will learn to treat wealth creation the way you treat clinical practice — **with a framework, a protocol, and the discipline to follow it consistently.**

1.8 — Two Doctors, Two Outcomes

Dr. Pradeep *Orthopaedic Surgeon · Bangalore* • Income: ₹3.5 lakh/month • Two investment flats • Fixed costs: ₹3.3 lakh/month • Savings in bank: ₹1.8 lakh	**Dr. Arvind** *Orthopaedic Surgeon · Visakhapatnam* • One home only • Fixed costs: ₹91,000/month • 14 months' expenses in liquid fund • Auto SIP: ₹75,000/month
COVID hit — had to borrow from a relative to pay staff.	**COVID hit — increased his SIPs. No borrowing needed.**

Same profession. Same specialty. Same pandemic. Radically different outcomes.

The difference was not income, intelligence, or effort. It was structure — and the deliberate decision to build it before it was needed.

1.9 — A Promise Before We Begin

In medicine, diagnosis precedes treatment. This book follows the same discipline.

What follows is a structured diagnosis of the financial life of an Indian doctor — the blind spots, the structural risks, and the frameworks to address them — so that wealth builds quietly, consistently, and without stress.

Because ultimately, wealth is not created by isolated decisions. It is created by seeing clearly — and then allowing time to do its work.

Chapter 2

The Doctor's Income–Expense Trap

Dr. Navya — Gynaecologist, Mysuru

Dr. Navya had been practising in Mysuru for seven years. Her income had grown from ₹1.4 lakh to ₹2.2 lakh a month. But her savings had quietly fallen from ₹35,000 to ₹12,000 a month — not through any crisis, but simply because expenses had expanded to fill everything her income had grown into.

Clinic upgrade. Better locality. Car EMI. Staff addition. A holiday that felt earned after years of grinding. Each decision reasonable. Each justified. Together, they had turned seven years of hard work into ₹12,000 a month in savings.

She had not noticed it happening. That was the most unsettling part.

2.1 — Earning Well Is Not the Same as Building Wealth

The question is not how much you earn. It is what your income is actually doing.

A doctor earning ₹25 lakh a year and saving 8% builds wealth more slowly than a schoolteacher earning ₹8 lakh and saving 30%. Income is the raw material. Wealth is what you build with it. Between the two sit structural forces — specific to medicine, predictable in effect, entirely addressable — that quietly consume the difference.

This chapter names those forces. Because you cannot fix what you have not seen.

2.2 — The Fixed Cost Burden

Every doctor carries two expense structures simultaneously — a household and a clinic — and neither pauses when income does.

- **Household** — EMI or rent, school fees, groceries, insurance, car, staff, utilities
- **Clinic** — rent, salaries, consumables, equipment maintenance, compliance

Together, these create a fixed monthly floor of **₹1.2–3.5 lakh** for most established doctors — regardless of how many patients walked in that month. Each lifestyle upgrade adds a new fixed layer. Unlike income, fixed costs rarely come down.

2.3 — Financial Arrhythmia

A doctor's income is flat through the long years of training, then climbs steeply once practice stabilises. *This curve — often called the J-Curve — is the defining shape of a doctor's financial journey.* Understanding it is the first step to working with it intelligently.

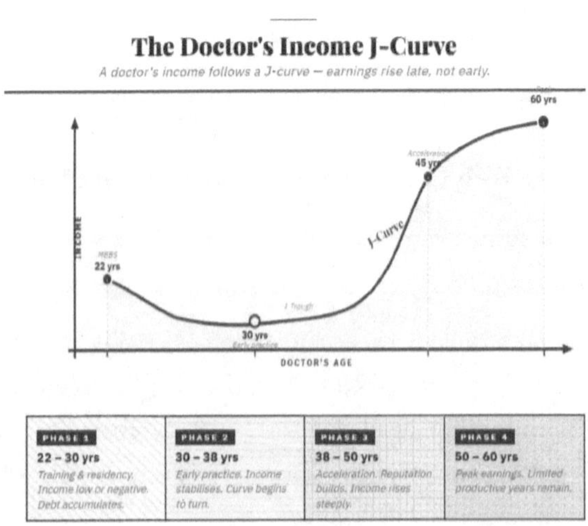

Figure 2.3 — The Doctor's Earning Curve: a long flat base through training, followed by a steep climb once practice stabilises.

The structural problem this creates:

Irregular income	**+**	**Fixed costs**	**=**	**Financial Arrhythmia**

OPD volumes shift with seasons. TPA reimbursements arrive late. A specialist's October income may be 40% higher than July — entirely outside their control. But the EMI goes out on the first. Staff salaries are due regardless of footfall.

The result: months that feel flush, months that feel suffocating. This rhythm pushes doctors toward decisions that feel safe but are damaging — FDs over equity, physical gold over diversified investments, property over liquidity. **Income stability does not come from earning more. It comes from a structure that buffers the volatility that is always going to be there.**

2.4 — The Invisible Spending Triggers

Three triggers specific to the profession drive the leak:

- **Guilt spending** — long hours and missed family time get compensated through purchases that feel like restitution
- **Peer comparison** — clinic refurbishments, cars, schools, and holidays circulate constantly through medical networks
- **Social signalling** — a doctor's visible lifestyle is read, fairly or not, as a proxy for clinical competence

The spending this produces is not careless. It is emotionally coherent — which is exactly what makes it invisible until the damage is done. *Chapter 7 addresses this in full.*

2.5 — Two Doctors, One Pattern

	Dr. Rajan — Endocrinologist, Coimbatore	**Dr. Suresh — Dermatologist, Pune**
Monthly income	₹3.8 lakh	₹3.2 lakh
Properties	3 (home + flat + plot)	1 (home only)
Fixed costs	~₹2.8 lakh/month	₹94,000/month
Liquid savings	₹1.5 lakh	11 months of expenses
When income dropped 40%	Borrowed from a colleague to pay staff	**Increased SIPs. Recovered without borrowing.**

Same city. Similar incomes. The difference was the structure underneath — not the earnings on top.

2.6 — The 3-Layer Solution

Wealth creation for doctors does not begin with investment products. It begins with three layers, built in sequence:

- **Layer 1 — Cash-flow infrastructure** — know exactly what comes in and goes out — clinic and household — every month. Separate accounts. Monthly review. Most doctors have a rough sense of their income and a rougher sense of their expenses. That gap is where the leak lives.
- **Layer 2 — Investment structure** — once cash flow is visible, surplus is directed deliberately — SIPs, liquid funds, REITs, hybrid funds — automated and sized to what actually exists, not what is hoped for.
- **Layer 3 — Behavioural discipline** — structure is itself protection. Automated investments happen before the emotional spending conversation begins. A liquidity buffer means a slow month does not force a bad decision.

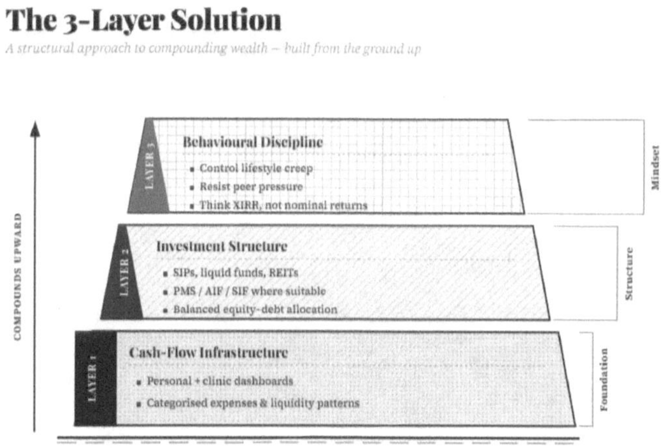

Figure 2.6 — The 3-Layer Solution: built from foundation upward. Each layer enables and protects the layer above it.

When all three layers are in place, wealth compounds quietly in the background while the clinical work continues.

2.7 — Before You Move On

If your income stopped for ninety days tomorrow — not permanently, just ninety days — would your investments still be running? Would your fixed costs be covered without borrowing?

If the answer is uncertain, that uncertainty is exactly what this book addresses — one layer at a time.

Chapter 3

Myths Doctors Commonly Believe

3.1 — Why Smart Doctors Fall for Bad Money Advice

Doctors are intelligent, disciplined, and trained to make high-stakes decisions. Yet with money, even accomplished specialists fall for beliefs with little factual basis.

Medicine trains the mind for precision. Finance is filled with noise. Under long hours and emotional pressure, doctors naturally seek safety, familiarity, and peer validation — instincts that serve well in clinical practice but become dangerous in investing.

This chapter dismantles nine myths using logic, data, and real-world outcomes.

3.2 — Myth 1: "Real Estate Always Doubles — and More Property Means More Wealth"

This belief was born during the 1998–2012 property boom — an era of cash transactions, opaque pricing, and rapid urbanisation. That world no longer exists.

Post-2015, RERA, demonetisation, increased supply, and greater transparency have fundamentally altered real estate economics. Growth today is largely linear, not exponential.

- Capital appreciation: 3–5%
- Rental yield: 2–3%
- Total return: 5–8% pre-tax

After costs, taxes, maintenance, and vacancy — real returns often fail to beat inflation. Yet doctors keep buying second and third properties, believing each adds wealth. In most cases, each adds EMI, illiquidity, and stress.

> **Any asset that cannot be exited quickly — without negotiation, legal friction, or a broker — is not an investment. It is an obligation.**

REITs, InvITs, and real-estate AIFs provide genuine real estate exposure without these burdens. Chapter 5 examines this in detail.

3.3 — Myth 2: "FDs Are Safe"

FDs feel safe because the principal does not fluctuate. But safety must be measured in real returns — not comfort.

For a doctor in the 30% tax bracket:

- FD return: ~6.5%
- Post-tax return: ~4.5%
- Doctor lifestyle inflation: 10–12%

The real return is negative. FDs are useful for emergency funds, short-term parking, and elderly dependents. They reduce discomfort — not financial disease. Chapter 4 calculates exactly what FD dependence costs over a decade.

3.4 — Myth 3: "Mutual Funds Are Risky; Equity Is Gambling"

Doctors often confuse volatility with risk. Real risk is illiquidity and unclear exits — seen in unlisted shares, closed-ended schemes, bundled insurance products, and undocumented lending.

Equity is volatile. It is also regulated, transparent, and liquid. Over any 10-year period in India, equity has never permanently destroyed disciplined long-term wealth.

> **Data doesn't lie. Emotions do.**

3.5 — Myth 4: "Insurance Is an Investment"

Insurance protects life. Investments grow money. Mixing the two creates poor insurance and poor returns.

ULIPs, endowments, money-back plans, and child plans persist because of emotional selling and tax framing — not because they work. Adequate term insurance combined with disciplined equity investing will always outperform bundled products over any meaningful horizon.

3.6 — Myth 5: "I'll Start Investing After My Loans Are Cleared"

This belief delays investing by a decade or more. Loans don't disappear sequentially — new ones replace old ones. Waiting for a clean slate postpones compounding indefinitely.

> SIPs should be treated as EMIs toward future freedom — just as education loans were EMIs toward career growth. **Both run in parallel with life. So should investing.**

3.7 — Myth 6: "Tax Saving Equals Financial Planning"

Doctors often invest for deductions rather than returns. Paying slightly more tax is better than locking capital into low-return, illiquid products for decades.

Section 80C has driven more wealth destruction among doctors than any market crash — through years of capital locked in endowments, ULIPs, and traditional plans that quietly underperformed.

Tax efficiency should support wealth creation. Not sabotage it.

3.8 — Myth 7: "I Don't Earn Enough to Invest"

Investing begins with habit — not surplus. A resident investing ₹5,000 a month builds discipline and compounding muscle long before income rises.

When income finally grows, obligations grow faster than intent. Those who built the habit early adjust upward effortlessly. Those who waited find it genuinely difficult to begin — not because of money, but because the habit was never formed.

3.9 — Myth 8: "My CA Will Handle Everything"

CAs are essential — for taxation, audits, and compliance. They are not trained in asset allocation, market cycles, liquidity planning, or the suitability of PMS, AIF, and SIF structures.

Doctors need both: a CA for tax and a wealth advisor for financial structure. These are different disciplines. Treating them as interchangeable is like asking a physician to perform surgery because both went to medical college.

A wrong financial product can quietly erase a decade of savings. A CA who recommended one is not liable. A wealth advisor who recommended one is.

3.10 — Myth 9: "I Avoid Risk — and I Know Enough to Manage My Own Money"

Two myths in one — and they often travel together.

On risk: wrong risk bleeds capital. No risk causes atrophy. Every return that exists anywhere was generated because someone took risk intelligently. Doctors who avoid all financial risk guarantee one outcome — that their purchasing power will steadily erode while they feel safe.

On self-management: education does not equal financial clarity. A cardiologist reading an ECG and a cardiologist reading a PMS term sheet are operating in entirely different terrains. One is trained. The other is not. The confidence that comes from medical expertise can be genuinely dangerous when applied to investment decisions made in fifteen minutes, under fatigue, after a long OPD.

Money demands time, emotional calm, structured thinking, and long-term discipline. This book is an attempt to provide the structure — so that self-management, where it happens, is at least informed.

3.11 — Four Doctors, Four Myths in Action

Dr. Prakash — Diabetologist, Karnal

Believed FDs were safe and avoided equity for ten years. His purchasing power quietly eroded while his bank balance nominally grew. Comfort stayed high. Wealth did not move.

Dr. Jeethu — Nephrologist, Kochi

Bought a second property believing real estate never fails. Eight years later the flat was illiquid, underperforming, and had a tenant in dispute. The paper value looked fine. The financial reality did not.

Dr. Ahmed — ENT, Mumbai

Avoided mutual funds because markets fell 30% once and scared him. He stayed in FDs. Equity recovered and compounded. His money did not. A temporary fall became a permanent opportunity loss.

Dr. Shreya — Homeopath, Indore

Waited until her education loan was cleared before investing. By then, twelve years of compounding had passed. She started late and invested well — but the first decade was gone permanently. Time, not returns, was the biggest cost.

Income was not the problem in any of these cases. Beliefs shaped decisions. Decisions shaped outcomes.

3.12 — Before You Move On

One question: *Of the nine myths in this chapter — how many have influenced a financial decision you made in the last two years?*

If the answer is more than one, the next chapter is especially important. It introduces the one measurement tool that cuts through every myth, every product pitch, and every well-meaning piece of advice from a colleague.

Chapter 4

Inflation, Real Returns & XIRR

The Only Truth That Matters in Investing

4.1 — Why This Chapter Changes Everything

Most doctors don't lose money in markets. They lose money by misunderstanding returns.

Statements like *"my property doubled in 8 years"* or *"my FD gives 7%"* or *"my policy gives a bonus every year"* mean nothing unless one question is answered: **what is the real return after inflation, tax, cost, liquidity, and time?**

If that real return is low — or negative — you are working harder while wealth stands still. This chapter trains you to see money the way you see a patient: objectively, without bias, and with the right investigation before drawing any conclusion.

4.2 — The Inflation Doctors Actually Face

Nominal inflation in India runs at approximately 5–6%. But doctors do not live a 5–6% inflation life.

Doctor lifestyle inflation runs at **10–12%** — because doctors spend disproportionately on housing upgrades, children's education, professional upkeep, clinic infrastructure, travel, and social obligations that come with the identity of being a doctor.

- **Professional inflation** — conferences, equipment upgrades, staff costs, clinic renovations, marketing
- **Personal inflation** — premium schooling, housing upgrades, travel, social events, healthcare for parents

> **You are not competing with CPI. You are competing with your own lifestyle inflation.** This is why doctors earning ₹25–50 lakh annually still feel financially stretched — their inflation rate is almost double the headline number.

4.3 — Inflation Erodes Corpus Silently

A corpus of ₹1 crore quietly loses real value every year it does not grow faster than inflation. At 10% inflation:

- After 5 years: ~₹59 lakh in real value
- After 10 years: ~₹35 lakh in real value
- After 15 years: ~₹21 lakh in real value

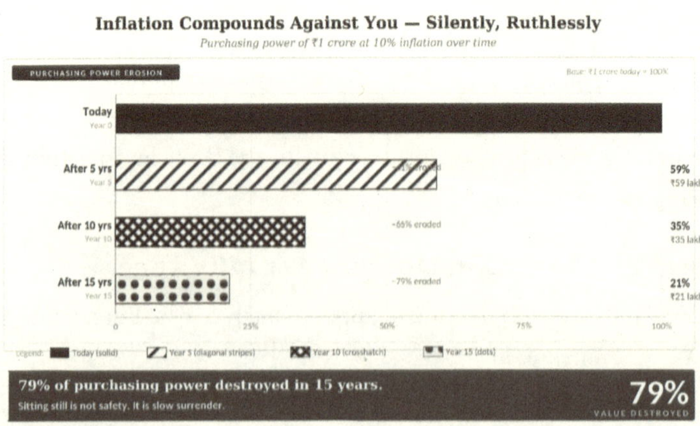

Figure 4.3 — At 10% inflation, a corpus that earns less than inflation loses more than half its real value in a decade. This is not market loss. This is erosion.

This is not market loss. The money is still there. The number may even be growing nominally. But its purchasing power — its ability to fund the life it was meant to fund — is disappearing year by year.

> **Inflation is the disease. Compounding is the cure.** If your investments don't beat inflation by at least 3–5% annually, you are losing money while believing you are safe.

4.4 — Nominal Return vs Real Return vs XIRR

There are three layers of truth in investing. Most doctors stop at the first.

Nominal return — what is advertised. *"FD gives 7%." "Property doubled." "AIF returned 20%."*

Real return — what you keep after inflation. Real Return = Nominal Return − Inflation. If FD returns 7% and inflation is 10%, real return is **−3%.**

XIRR — the true annual return, adjusted for timing, cash flows, taxes, costs, and exit friction. It captures when money went in and came out, taxes paid, costs and exit loads, time lost in illiquid assets, and delays in receiving proceeds.

> **XIRR is the ECG of your investment. Everything else is noise.**
>
> Just as an ECG reveals what is actually happening inside the heart — not what the patient feels — XIRR reveals what is actually happening inside an investment. Once you start reading XIRR, every product pitch, every colleague's success story, and every return claim becomes instantly testable.

4.5 — The FD Calculation Doctors Ignore

For a doctor in the 30% tax bracket:

- FD rate: 7%
- Post-tax return: 4.9%
- Doctor lifestyle inflation: 10%
- Real return: −5.1%

₹10 lakh in an FD over 10 years:

	Value
Nominal value	₹19.6 lakh
Post-tax value	₹15.5 lakh
Real value (after 10% inflation)	**₹6.9 lakh**

The number doubled. The wealth did not. In real terms, ₹10 lakh became ₹6.9 lakh — a loss of ₹3.1 lakh in purchasing power despite a growing bank balance. This is why FDs are hazardous when used beyond their proper purpose — emergency funds and short-term parking.

4.6 — Real Estate: The Principle

A doctor buys a flat for ₹60 lakh. Sells it for ₹1.2 crore in 8 years. The money doubled — it looks like success. But after stamp duty, maintenance, repairs, vacancy, and brokerage, the XIRR is approximately 7.8%. Against 10% doctor inflation, the real return is negative. Chapter 5 works through this calculation in full detail.

> **The principle to carry from here:** nominal profit is not the same as real gain. XIRR is the only honest measure.

4.7 — Asset Class Real Returns: The Full Picture

Long-term Indian data on real returns (assuming 10% inflation):

Asset Class	Nominal Returns (15–20 yrs)	Real Return After 10% Inflation	Liquidity	Transparency
FD	6–7%	−1% to 0%	High	High
Gold	8–9%	~1%	Medium	High
Physical Real Estate	5–8%	−1% to +1%	Low	Low
REITs / InvITs	8–12%	2–6%	High	High
Debt Funds	7–9%	0–2%	High	High
Equity Funds	12–16%	5–10%	High	High
PMS / AIF Cat III	14–22%	7–15%	Medium	Medium
SIF	14–20%	7–12%	Medium	High

Assets with **liquidity + transparency + growth** deliver the highest real returns over time. The pattern is consistent across every market cycle.

4.8 — Liquidity and Exit: The Forgotten Variables

Doctors rarely lose money on returns alone. They lose significantly on illiquidity, time, and exit costs.

Investment	Typical Exit Time	Exit Cost	Liquidity Issues
Real Estate	3–24 months	3–12% (stamp duty + brokerage)	Legal risks, opaque pricing
PMS / AIF	30–90 days	~1% within load period	Lock-ins, structure-based exits
Mutual Funds	1–3 working days	~1% within load period	High liquidity, transparent
REITs / InvITs	T+2 days	Nil	Listed, no hassles
SIFs	Equity ~3 days Hybrid ~15 days	Max 1%	Regulated, transparent

> **Liquidity is not about returns.** It is about choice, dignity, and sleep.

4.9 — Opportunity Cost: The Silent Killer

Every rupee stuck in a low-return investment loses its potential permanently.

Investment	Value after 10 years
₹20 lakh in FD @ 7%	₹39 lakh
₹20 lakh in Equity @ 15%	**₹81 lakh**
Lost opportunity	₹42 lakh

That ₹42 lakh was never lost to a market crash. It was lost to a decision that felt safe. Doctors underestimate opportunity cost more than almost any other profession — because the loss is invisible, produces no statement, and generates no alarm.

4.10 — Two Doctors, One Decade, Two Outcomes

Dr. Sriram — Orthopaedic Surgeon, Faridabad

In 2014, invested ₹50 lakh into a residential property — his "safest" option. By 2023 it sold for ₹80 lakh. After costs, the XIRR was approximately 5.4%. Against 10% inflation, the real return was negative. Nine years of capital produced a nominal gain and a real loss.

Dr. Sunil — General Surgeon, Hyderabad

In 2014, invested the same ₹50 lakh into a diversified flexi-cap equity fund. By 2023 it had grown to approximately ₹2.09 crore — an XIRR of ~18.25%, delivering around 8% positive real return after inflation. The money created liquidity, flexibility, and compounding that continued working after the investment was made.

Same starting point. Same amount. Same decade. The only difference was the question each doctor asked about their returns.

Dr. Sriram asked: "Did it grow?"

Dr. Sunil asked: "What did it actually earn — after everything?"

Stop asking how much it grew. Start asking what it really earned.

4.11 — One Principle to Carry Forward

"Wealth without inflation-beating returns is like untreated hypertension — no symptoms today, catastrophic consequences later. The damage accumulates silently, and by the time it shows, years of opportunity are already lost."

You need **growth + liquidity + inflation-adjusted returns** — all three, consistently, over time. XIRR is the instrument that tells you whether you have them.

4.12 — Before You Move On

One habit from this chapter onward:

Before accepting any return figure — from a salesman, a colleague, or your own calculation — ask: what is the XIRR? What is the real return after inflation? Can I exit when I need to?

If those three questions cannot be answered clearly, the investment cannot be evaluated honestly.

Chapter 5

How Doctors Get Stuck in Real Estate

5.1 — The Dominant Trap

If there is one asset class that dominates the financial lives of Indian doctors and silently shapes their net worth, it is real estate.

Every doctor has a story — the plot that was going to double in five years, the builder's pre-launch deal that a colleague passed on and regretted, the second flat that was going to generate rental income. Real estate runs on emotion, reinforced by culture, peer validation, and a generational memory of extraordinary returns.

It is also the single biggest reason why doctors struggle with liquidity, flexibility, and compounding. Not because real estate is inherently bad — but because doctors consistently get **overexposed and underinformed.** This chapter shows how the trap forms, what it actually costs, and how to hold real estate intelligently without damaging everything else.

5.2 — Why Doctors Are Drawn to Real Estate

Six psychological triggers drive this concentration:

- **Tangibility bias** — land and buildings feel real in a way a portfolio statement does not
- **Healthcare analogy bias** — "hospitals are expanding here, so prices must rise" — plausible, but rarely as reliable as it sounds
- **Overconfidence in local knowledge** — "I know this area" — sometimes true, more often misleading
- **Peer validation** — when everyone in the medical circle is buying, hesitation feels like a mistake

- **Social expectation** — property signals arrival; a second flat signals success
- **Generational memory** — returns of 15–25% CAGR between 1998 and 2012 are still the mental anchor, even though that era is gone

This combination leads not to diversification — but to concentration.

5.3 — The Era Doctors Remember vs the Era They Are In

The 1998–2012 period created a generational illusion. Urbanisation was exploding, IT incomes were surging, cash dominated transactions, supply was limited, and regulation was absent. In that environment, 15–25% CAGR returns were achievable — often fuelled by speculative demand and undisclosed cash.

That era is over.

Post-2015, RERA enforces accountability, GST adds to costs, supply is abundant, and buyers are far better informed. Growth today is largely linear, not exponential. The doctor who anchors expectations on 1998–2012 data and applies them to a 2025 purchase is making a decision based on a market that no longer exists.

5.4 — Hidden Risks Doctors Consistently Underestimate

Beyond returns, real estate carries six structural risks that most doctors do not fully price in before buying:

- **Liquidity** — exit can take 3 to 24 months; in a distressed sale, longer
- **Legal** — title defects, boundary disputes, encroachments, and tenant complications can freeze capital for years with no resolution in sight
- **Builder risk** — delays, project cancellations, and insolvency are not rare; RERA helps but does not eliminate them

- **Concentration** — when 70–80% of net worth sits in a single asset class, a slowdown in that class is not a portfolio problem — it is a personal financial crisis
- **Opportunity cost** — every rupee locked in a 6% XIRR property is a rupee not compounding at 14–16% in equity
- **Maintenance and vacancy** — recurring outflows that quietly erode returns year after year without appearing in any headline number

Real estate is not a bad asset. **Overexposure to it is.**

5.5 — The Calculation Doctors Never Do

"I bought a flat for ₹80 lakh in 2015 and sold it for ₹1.6 crore in 2024. It doubled."

This is the sentence most doctors use to describe a property investment. It sounds like success. Here is what the numbers actually show.

Scenario A — Cash Purchase

Total outflows: ₹80L purchase + ₹6.4L stamp duty + ₹2.7L maintenance + ₹2L repairs + ₹1.6L brokerage on exit = ₹92.7L deployed over 9 years.

Net in-hand after sale: ₹67.3L gain on ₹92.7L deployed.

XIRR: 6.5%. Real return after 10% doctor inflation: **−3.5%**

Scenario B — Loan Purchase (80% LTV at 8.5%)

Down payment ₹16L + stamp duty ₹6.4L. EMI ₹55,540/month. Over 9 years, total EMIs paid: ₹60L, of which ₹43.5L was pure interest. Outstanding loan at sale: ₹47.5L — repaid from proceeds.

Total cash out: ₹87L. Net in-hand after repaying loan: ₹110.9L.

XIRR: 4.3%. Real return after 10% inflation: **−5.7%**

Scenario C — With Rental Income (2% yield)

Annual rent ₹1.6L, post-tax ₹1.12L/year. Total rental income over 9 years: ₹10.1L net. Even adding rental income, XIRR rises only to 7.5%.

> **Real return with rent: −2.5%.** Every scenario is negative in real terms.

	Scenario A Cash Purchase	Scenario B Loan Purchase	Scenario C With Rental
XIRR	6.5%	4.3%	7.5%
Real return (after 10% inflation)	**−3.5%**	**−5.7%**	**−2.5%**

Important note on Scenario B: the loan appears to generate a higher rupee return (₹83.8L net) than cash (₹67.3L). This is leverage at work. But the doctor paid ₹43.5L in interest to earn that extra ₹16.5L. XIRR tells the true story: 4.3%.

> **The comparison that never gets made:** ₹80 lakh invested in a diversified flexi-cap equity fund in 2015 at 15% CAGR would have grown to **₹2.81 crore by 2024** — fully liquid, zero maintenance, no brokerage, no legal risk. Against the property's gross proceeds of ₹1.6 crore, the equity advantage is **₹1.21 crore of additional corpus.** Most doctors never calculate this — because EMIs hide the true cost, and the nominal doubling feels like success.

5.6 — How Doctors Get Overexposed

The pattern is almost always the same:

- First home — emotional necessity, usually justified
- Second property — "investment"
- Third plot — "future plan" or "for the children"

By this point, 70–90% of net worth is locked in real estate. Liquidity is negligible. Emergency cushion is thin. EMIs are high. And stress is rising — quietly, steadily, exactly the way a slow-growing problem presents before it becomes a crisis.

The pain does not appear immediately. It surfaces between ages 45 and 55 — when income volatility rises, children's education costs peak, and the properties that were supposed to fund retirement are illiquid, underperforming, and expensive to hold.

5.7 — Geography Shapes the Mistake

The trap looks different depending on where the doctor practises, but the outcome is the same:

- **Tier-1 cities (Mumbai, Delhi NCR, Bengaluru)** — high prices, low rental yields of 2–3%, capital appreciation that has barely kept pace with inflation post-2015
- **Tier-2 cities (Hyderabad, Pune, Chennai)** — peer pressure and relationship-driven deals from builders and brokers who know doctors have capital and trust colleagues
- **Tier-3 cities (Coimbatore, Kochi, Indore)** — speculative agricultural and residential plots with no rental income, illiquid exits, and documentation risks

Different geographies. Different entry prices. Same outcome: illiquidity.

5.8 — The Alternative: Financial Real Estate

Doctors do not need to eliminate real estate exposure. They need to access it differently.

REITs and InvITs — listed on stock exchanges, SEBI-regulated — offer distribution yields of 7–8% plus 2–5% capital appreciation, entry from ₹10,000, exit in 2 working days, and no tenants, no maintenance, no legal complications, and no brokerage. This is real estate stripped of its structural problems.

For appreciation without speculation, Category II Real Estate AIFs offer professionally managed portfolios with targeted returns of 12–18%, defined exit timelines, and institutional-grade due diligence — replacing land gambling with structured growth.

The old era was land and buildings. The new era is financial real estate.

5.9 — Four Doctors, Two Patterns

Dr. Manoharan — Neurosurgeon, Chennai

Bought four properties over 12 years. EMIs consumed cash flow; rent covered less than half. No emergency fund, no equity exposure. When a slowdown in surgical referrals reduced income for eight months, the properties offered nothing — they could not be partially liquidated, could not be mortgaged quickly, and the rent barely covered maintenance. He had assets. He had no options.

Dr. Kiran — Orthopaedic Surgeon, Chandigarh

Owned one home and used REITs and InvITs instead of a second flat. Maintained 12 months of expenses in liquid funds, equity exposure through SIPs. During a clinic disruption, her portfolio continued working. She did not panic, did not sell, and did not borrow.

Same surgical specialty tier. Same city tier. The difference was what the second rupee of surplus went into.

Dr. Harisha — Diabetologist, Cuttack

Bought land across three locations between 2012 and 2018 — no rental income, only appreciation hopes. When a family medical emergency needed ₹8 lakh urgently in 2021, none of the three plots could be liquidated in time. Documentation on one was in dispute. A second was jointly held and needed a co-seller's signatures. He borrowed from a colleague at 18% for six months.

Dr. Yashoda — Nephrologist, Baroda

Owned one home and allocated surplus across equity SIPs, one REIT, and a Category II AIF. When a similar emergency arose, she redeemed from her liquid fund the same afternoon. Her equity portfolio and AIF were untouched. The emergency cost her nothing in opportunity — only in money, which was the point of having it liquid.

Same clinical specialty tier. Same income range. The difference was that one had wealth that could be accessed, and one had wealth that could only be admired.

5.10 — The Framework

Two rules that prevent the trap:

> **Rule 1 — If you cannot exit easily, do not enter easily.** Every property purchase deserves one honest question before signing: how long would this take to sell, at what discount, and under what conditions? If the answer is uncomfortable, the purchase deserves more scrutiny.
>
> **Rule 2 — Real estate should not exceed 25–30% of net worth.** This includes the home you live in. Beyond this threshold, concentration risk dominates. Below it, real estate can play its legitimate role — stability, inflation hedge, emotional anchor — without damaging everything else.

With REITs, InvITs, and Cat-II AIFs already available, there is no need to take on physical property's structural costs to get real estate exposure. The exposure exists. The damage does not have to.

5.11 — Before You Move On

Add up your current real estate exposure — home, investment properties, plots, and land. What percentage of your total net worth does it represent?

If the answer exceeds 40%, the remaining chapters of this book will require one prior decision: to gradually rebalance toward liquid, income-generating assets. Everything else builds on that foundation.

Chapter 6

Wealth Drivers for Doctors

6.1 — Wealth Creation Is Not a Mystery. It Is a Structure.

Every doctor seeks freedom — financial, professional, and psychological. Freedom from constant financial stress, social pressure, and anxiety about retirement.

Yet most doctors still believe wealth is created by higher income, more patients, and longer hours. That belief is incomplete.

> **Income enables wealth. It does not create it.**

Wealth is created only when surplus is invested correctly and allowed to compound over time. This chapter explains the eight engines that decide how fast — and how sustainably — a doctor's net worth grows.

6.2 — Driver 1: India's Compounding Decade

Doctors practising in India today are operating in an unusually favourable window. India is not just growing — it is structurally compounding.

India is approaching a \$5 trillion economy and moving toward the third largest in the world by the early 2030s. Per-capita income is crossing the \$2,500–3,000 threshold — the zone where, historically, consumption accelerates, financial markets deepen, and corporate earnings grow faster than the economy itself.

The impact on doctors is direct and dual:

- Rising discretionary healthcare spend — more elective procedures, better insurance penetration, stronger hospital economics
- Deeper, better-regulated capital markets — equity, REITs, InvITs, SIFs, GIFT City platforms — giving doctors access to asset classes unavailable a decade ago

Developed markets grow at 1–3%. India grows at 7–8%+. **Doctors benefit twice — through rising income and through the compounding of investments inside a growing economy.**

This is a rare convergence decade. Doctors who build the right financial structure now will compound alongside India's growth. Those who delay will watch this window narrow.

6.3 — Driver 2: Surplus — The Fuel of Wealth

Doctors ask: "How much should I invest?" The better question is: "How much surplus can I generate consistently?"

Surplus = Income − Lifestyle − Commitments

Increase surplus + Invest surplus + Protect surplus = Wealth

Most doctors struggle not because income is low, but because lifestyle expands faster than income. Every clinic upgrade, car change, and school fee increase is a permanent reduction in surplus. For wealth to compound, surplus must grow, be protected from emotional spending, and be automated into investments before it disappears.

A doctor saving 30% of income consistently can reach financial independence in 15–18 years — even without extraordinary returns. The percentage matters more than the absolute amount.

6.4 — Driver 3: Asset Allocation — The Compounding Engine

Once surplus is created, allocation matters more than the amount invested. Asset allocation determines whether compounding accelerates or stagnates.

A typical doctor portfolio is heavy on real estate and FDs, some gold, minimal equity, and poor liquidity. The result: low real returns, high stress, and limited flexibility.

What financially stable doctors do differently is not product selection — it is allocation structure. A recommended strategic framework for doctors:

- **Equity (mutual funds, PMS, AIF Cat III, SIFs)** — 30–50%
- **Real estate (home + REITs + Cat II AIFs)** — 20–30%
- **Debt (short-duration funds, liquid funds)** — 10–20%
- **Gold and Silver ETFs** — 5–10%
- **Liquidity buffer** — 5–10%

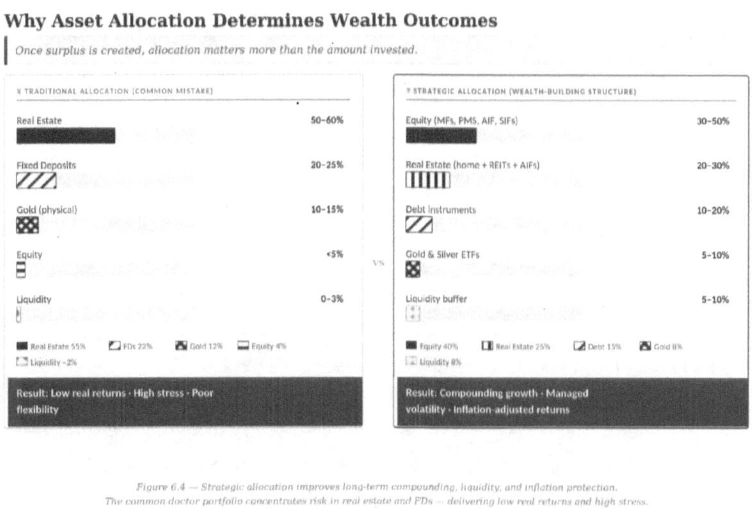

Figure 6.4 — Strategic allocation improves long-term compounding, liquidity, and inflation protection. The common doctor portfolio concentrates risk in real estate and FDs — delivering low real returns and high stress.

Once allocation is correct, product selection becomes a secondary optimisation — not the primary driver of wealth.

6.5 — Driver 4: Compounding — The Silent Multiplier

Compounding is deceptive. After a decade of investing ₹25,000 per month at 12% return, the corpus is only ₹58 lakh. Many lose patience here — and stop.

But compounding works silently before it works dramatically.

Between Years 20 and 30, the same portfolio jumps from ₹2.5 crore to ₹8.8 crore. The last decade creates more wealth than the first two combined.

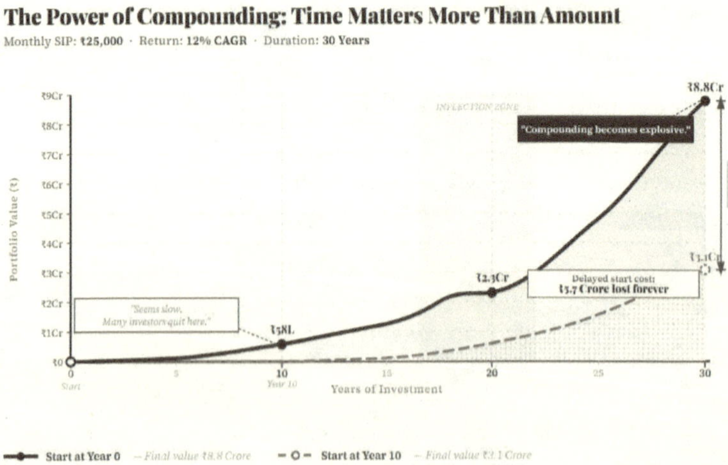

Figure 6.5 — The real power of compounding appears late. Starting just 10 years late reduces the final corpus from ₹8.8 crore to ₹2.5 crore — a permanent ₹6.3 crore cost for one decade of delay.

Compounding rewards time more than effort. Starting early is its only true requirement.

The corollary is equally important: staying invested matters as much as starting. A doctor who starts early but stops SIPs during every market correction forfeits most of the benefit. Wealth grows the same way clinical skill improves — through consistency, not intensity.

6.6 — Driver 5: Quality of Investments

Not all investments compound equally. The same corpus in two different instruments over 20 years can produce a difference of several crore — purely from product quality.

- **Wealth destroyers** — ULIPs and endowments, unlisted broker-sold shares, overpriced property, builder pre-launch traps, unregulated instruments
- **Wealth accelerators** — equity mutual funds, PMS, Category II and III AIFs, SIFs, REITs and InvITs, international and GIFT City funds

The diagnostic tool that separates the two is always XIRR. Every product that cannot demonstrate a clear, favourable XIRR over a sufficient time horizon belongs in the first list.

6.7 — Driver 6: Liquidity — The Oxygen of Wealth

Doctors face unpredictable demands — medical emergencies, clinic relocations, family responsibilities, and market opportunities that require capital quickly. Liquidity provides negotiating power, peace of mind, and dignity under pressure.

Without liquidity, even wealthy doctors feel trapped. Debt becomes the default response to every need. Forced asset sales happen at the worst possible time. Stress becomes chronic.

Liquidity does not reduce returns. It prevents forced mistakes.

A 12-month expense buffer in a liquid fund is not idle money. It is the foundation that allows every other driver to function without interruption.

6.8 — Driver 7: The Right Advisor

No doctor operates alone in the OT. Yet many attempt to manage significant wealth in isolation — relying on a CA's product recommendations, a banker's suggestions, or a colleague's tip.

A competent wealth advisor provides asset allocation, risk management, entry and exit discipline, product suitability assessment, and the behavioural guardrails that prevent panic decisions. An additional 3–4% annual alpha through disciplined allocation and rebalancing, sustained over 20 years, translates into crores — not percentages.

Professional guidance compounds wealth. Going solo risks compounding financial errors.

6.9 — Driver 8: Behavioural Discipline

Even the best-constructed portfolio fails under poor behaviour. The most common behavioural mistakes among doctors:

- Stopping SIPs during market corrections — precisely when more should be going in
- Panic redemptions after a 20–30% drawdown — locking in losses permanently
- Buying property under family or peer pressure, bypassing all financial logic
- Chasing last year's best-performing product — entering at the top

Stable behaviour produces stable outcomes. Behavioural turbulence destroys returns faster than any market correction does.

6.10 — A Simple Wealth Framework for Doctors

Seven actions, applied consistently:

1. **Control lifestyle creep** — protect surplus before it is spent
2. **Build 9–12 months of liquidity** — clinic volatility demands this, not 6 months
3. **Automate surplus into SIPs and STPs** — remove the decision from the equation
4. **Allocate across equity, debt, alternatives, gold, and cash** — structure before products
5. **Protect with term, health, and professional indemnity insurance** — non-negotiable
6. **Track XIRR, not emotions** — the number tells the truth
7. **Stay invested through cycles** — time in the market, not timing the market

6.11 — Three Doctor Patterns

Dr. Amitabh — Haematologist, Pune

Lifestyle was rising faster than savings. His SIP had been stuck at ₹40,000 for four years despite income growth. He committed to a fixed savings rate and stepped up to ₹85,000 a month. Within five years, net worth accelerated — without a single additional hour of work. Surplus scaled. Wealth followed.

Dr. Pallavi — Endocrinologist, Hubli

Two early properties had consumed her surplus and crushed liquidity. She paused further property buying, built a 12-month buffer, and redirected surplus into REITs and a Category II AIF. Stress reduced, liquidity returned, and her portfolio became structured enough to think about an SWP within a decade. The reallocation cost her nothing in returns — only the social validation of owning more property.

Dr. Sunil and Dr. Deepa — Doctor Couple, Ahmedabad

High combined income, but fragmented SIPs, overlapping funds, and no coherent allocation logic. They consolidated into a joint framework with defined goals, annual rebalancing, and XIRR tracking. Volatility reduced. Goal clarity improved. The portfolio began working as a system rather than a collection of individual decisions.

In all three cases, the income was never the problem. Structure was.

6.12 — Before You Move On

Of the eight wealth drivers in this chapter — which ones are currently working in your financial life, and which ones are absent?

The ones that are absent are the answer to why income and net worth have not kept pace with each other.

Chapter 7

Lifestyle Creep & Expense Management for Doctors

7.1 — The Silent Disease That Attacks Doctor Wealth

In medicine, the most dangerous diseases are often the quiet ones — slow, painless, and ignored until damage becomes irreversible. Lifestyle creep behaves the same way. It is silent, progressive, emotionally driven, socially reinforced, and financially corrosive.

Doctors rarely struggle because of low income. They struggle because expenses rise faster than income — steadily, invisibly, and in ways that feel entirely reasonable at every step.

This chapter is not about frugality. It is about diagnosing a condition that most doctors don't realise they have.

7.2 — Why Doctors Are Uniquely Vulnerable

Doctors face a combination of pressures that few professions experience simultaneously:

1. **Delayed gratification** — after 10–15 years of training, there is a powerful urge to finally live well
2. **Sudden income acceleration** — doctor incomes jump sharply, not gradually, triggering immediate upgrades

3. **Social expectations** — doctors are expected to look successful, live in the right localities, and educate children at premium institutions

4. **Peer comparison** — subtle but constant comparisons with senior consultants, NRI relatives, and colleagues abroad

5. **Guilt-driven spending** — long hours and missed family time get compensated through money

Doctors don't overspend because they are careless. They overspend because the ecosystem nudges them continuously in that direction.

7.3 — The Lifestyle Escalation Curve

Most doctors follow a predictable four-phase trajectory:

Phase 1 (Age 28–32) — Income finally begins:

- Bike → Car · Basic rent → Better rent · Domestic → International travel

Phase 2 (Age 32–38) — Settling down:

- Home loan · Car loan · Equipment upgrades · Weddings & family events

Phase 3 (Age 38–45) — Family & responsibility:

- Children's education · Larger home · Bigger car · Social obligations

Phase 4 (Age 45–55) — Status cementing:

- Investment property · Home upgrades · Destination holidays
- Income stabilises. Expenses harden. Stress rises.

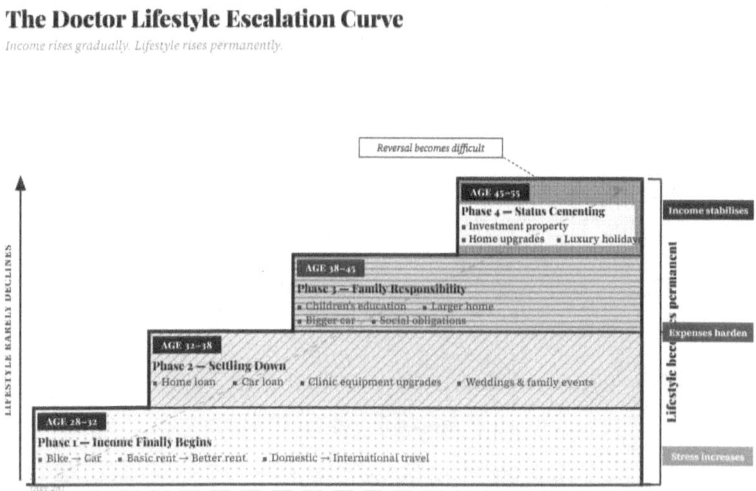

Figure 7.3 — Lifestyle rises in irreversible steps. As income stabilises, expenses harden and financial flexibility declines.

Lifestyle inflation rarely feels dangerous while it is happening. But it permanently limits future freedom.

7.4 — Expenses Become Fixed, Not Flexible

Most doctors believe they will control expenses later. In reality, lifestyle upgrades are almost never reversible.

- Bigger home → permanent EMI
- Better school → annual fee escalation
- Premium car → higher insurance, maintenance, and expectation of the next upgrade
- Better locality → fixed society charges that don't pause when income slows

Once comfort becomes the baseline, downgrading feels like deprivation. Households become addicted to a standard of living that was once optional but now feels essential.

7.5 — The Psychology Behind Lifestyle Creep

Five recurring justifications fuel the problem:

1. **"I deserve this."** — Emotionally valid. Financially dangerous when applied to every increment.
2. **"Everyone around me is doing it."** — Comparison erodes discipline faster than any market crash.
3. **"This is normal for my profession."** — Often untrue, almost always overstated.
4. **"This is for my family."** — Used to justify upgrades that exceed necessity and disguise guilt spending.
5. **"It's just an EMI."** — Small individually. Collectively suffocating.

7.6 — One Doctor, One Pattern

Dr. Keerthi — Consultant Radiologist, Hyderabad

Income: ₹3.2 lakh/month. Lifestyle: premium rent, car EMI, domestic help, frequent travel. Savings: ₹18,000/month.

She wasn't reckless — she was simply matching expenses to income. When hospital shifts reduced for six months, stress escalated rapidly. Once expenses rise, savings don't just fall. They disappear.

7.7 — The Lifestyle Creep Equation

Creep intensifies when: income growth is sudden, emotional spending is high, social pressure is constant.

Creep weakens when: financial awareness is strong and discipline is automated — not left to willpower.

You cannot control how fast income grows or how much peer pressure exists. You can control awareness and automation.

7.8 — The Lifestyle Lock + Automate Strategy

The rule: freeze lifestyle for three years when income rises. Direct every increment into investments, not upgrades.

- Step up SIPs immediately — before the increment gets absorbed
- Do not upgrade car, house, or holiday standard
- Automate everything: SIPs on income date, emergency fund sweep, REIT/InvIT standing instructions

> **Automation removes emotion from money.** Discipline through systems outlasts discipline through willpower every time.

Doctors who apply this rule achieve financial independence 5–10 years earlier than peers with comparable income.

7.9 — The Doctor's 50–30–20 Rule

Standard budgeting models don't fit a doctor's life. A more realistic structure:

- **50% — Needs** — home, EMIs, family, clinic fixed costs
- **20% — Wants** — travel, upgrades, lifestyle, discretionary
- **30% — Investments** — minimum, non-negotiable, automated

This is the standard rule — inverted. Most versions assign 20% to savings. For doctors, that number must be 30%. The lifestyle is already generously funded at 50%. The investment floor is what converts income into independence.

7.10 — The 4-Bucket Framework

- **Bucket 1 — Core Fixed** — home or rent, utilities, staff salaries, clinic rent
- **Bucket 2 — Lifestyle** — shopping, travel, gadgets, dining. If this crosses 20–25% of income, lifestyle creep is active.

- **Bucket 3 — Growth** — courses, skill upgrades, clinic improvements — investment in the income engine
- **Bucket 4 — Wealth Creation** — SIPs, REITs, InvITs, hybrid funds, PMS, AIF, SIF — the only bucket that compounds. Automate and protect.

7.11 — The True Cost of a Prestige Purchase

The first 5–7 years after stable income begins determine the entire compounding trajectory. Prestige purchases during this window remove capital at its highest-leverage point.

A doctor buys a **₹35 lakh** luxury car early in practice:

₹35 lakh invested at 15% for 10 years → **~₹1.4 crore**

Car resale in 10 years → ₹6–8 lakh | **Net wealth cost: over ₹1 crore**

Luxury earned costs money. Luxury borrowed costs freedom.

7.12 — Two Doctors, One Pattern

Dr. Ramya — Endocrinologist, Guntur

Upgrades became automatic as practice grew. Savings stayed below 8% despite rising income. After a 6-month lifestyle lock and SIP step-up, investments nearly quadrupled in three years. Income unchanged. Direction of surplus changed.

Dr. Meena — Neonatologist, Jaipur

Expenses felt reasonable until the 4-bucket framework revealed lifestyle costs above 30% and stagnant investing. Within a year of structured categorisation, expense volatility reduced and investments stabilised. Structure restored control faster than sacrifice.

Same profession. Same income tier. Both clinical specialists. The difference was the moment each chose to look at the numbers honestly.

7.13 — The Lifestyle Audit

Five questions — answer honestly:

1. Are EMIs above 30% of monthly income?
2. Do expenses rise automatically with every income increase?
3. Do I spend to compensate for stress, guilt, or missed family time?
4. Do I compare my lifestyle with peers and feel pressure to match it?
5. Has my investment percentage stayed flat for more than two years despite income growth?

Three or more yes answers indicate active lifestyle creep. The treatment is not sacrifice — it is structure, automation, and the lifestyle lock applied before the next increment arrives.

Chapter 8

The Psychology of Money for the Medical Mind

8.1 — Why Doctors Need a Different Money Psychology

Doctors are trained to observe, diagnose, reason, and rely on evidence. Bias is identified, questioned, and corrected in clinical practice. Yet when money enters the picture, many doctors abandon these very principles — not because they lack intelligence, but because financial decisions happen under fatigue, pressure, emotion, and social expectation.

Doctors receive no formal financial training, operate under chronic cognitive overload, face unpredictable income cycles, carry pressure to look successful, and postpone learning finance due to time scarcity.

> **Psychology — not income — is the strongest predictor of long-term wealth.** This chapter recalibrates the mental lens through which doctors view money.

8.2 — Rational in the Clinic, Emotional with Money

The contrast is striking and uncomfortable:

In medicine: evidence over anecdote • data over opinion • protocol over instinct • emotion separated from diagnosis.

In finance: peer opinions feel credible • social media advice feels convincing • fear overrides probability • losses feel personal • real estate feels safe • equity feels dangerous.

The same mind that demands scientific rigour in the clinic switches to emotional reasoning with money. Investing deals in probability, not certainty — and this mismatch creates predictable, repeatable errors.

8.3 — Five Psychological Traps Doctors Fall Into

1. Overconfidence Bias

Clinical competence spills into financial overconfidence. *"I can time the market." "I know this area will appreciate." "I don't need an advisor."* This leads doctors toward speculative land deals, unlisted shares without due diligence, and poorly timed market entries.

2. Loss Aversion

Medicine teaches *primum non nocere* — avoid harm first. In investing, this becomes intolerance to volatility, premature exits, avoidance of equity, and preference for assets that "don't fall" — FDs and property. The outcome: low real returns, inflation erosion, and weak compounding.

Avoiding volatility often creates the highest long-term risk.

3. Confirmation Bias

Doctors seek evidence to reinforce existing beliefs. Real estate believers ignore liquidity data. Equity sceptics focus only on crashes. FD believers ignore negative real returns. Confirmation bias locks portfolios into mediocrity.

6. Social Proof Bias

If enough doctors do something, it feels safe — buying multiple properties, joining land syndicates, following the same advisor, engaging in F&O without understanding. **Popularity substitutes for correctness.**

5. The Ego Problem

Doctors are uncomfortable saying *"I don't know."* This leads to avoiding questions, resisting advisors, and repeating the same mistakes in different packaging.

Ego protects professional identity — but damages financial outcomes.

8.4 — Why Doctors Prefer Tangible Over Financial Assets

Three reasons, all psychological:

- **Emotional comfort** — property feels solid, gold feels valuable, FDs feel stable. Equity feels invisible and volatile. Yet over long horizons, equity is safer than most physical assets.
- **Family and cultural pressure** — families push real estate. No one pressures a doctor to buy a diversified equity fund.
- **Zero learning curve** — FDs need no effort. Gold needs no analysis. Real estate runs on belief, not data. Equity demands learning, patience, and discipline — scarce resources for overworked doctors.

8.5 — How the Medical Profession Amplifies Financial Errors

Six profession-specific factors worsen financial behaviour:

1. **Emotional fatigue** → convenience-driven decisions
2. **Decision overload** → avoidance of financial thinking altogether
3. **Irregular income** → defensive, underinvested portfolios
4. **High responsibility** → exaggerated fear of financial risk
5. **Guilt-driven spending** → emotional purchases that bypass logic
6. **Identity pressure** → lifestyle commitments beyond financial necessity

The profession itself pushes doctors toward conservative, illiquid, low-return choices. Recognising this is the first step to counteracting it.

8.6 — Lessons from Behavioural Finance

Five principles every doctor must internalise:

- **Volatility is not risk** — permanent loss is. Short-term fluctuation in a well-chosen fund is the price of long-term return — not danger.

- **Illiquidity is risk** — even when prices don't fluctuate. A property that cannot be sold in three months carries real risk, regardless of paper value.
- **Emotion lowers XIRR** — every panic exit, every delayed entry, every product chosen for comfort rather than return shows up in the final number.
- **Time multiplies returns** — no product selection, no tactical shift, and no advisor can replicate what starting ten years earlier would have done.
- **Behaviour matters more than products** — a mediocre investment held with discipline outperforms a great investment abandoned at the first correction.

> *"A mediocre investment with good behaviour outperforms a great investment with poor discipline."*

8.7 — The Mindset Shifts That Change Everything

Seven beliefs that separate doctors who build wealth from those who don't:

1. XIRR matters more than stories
2. Inflation is the real enemy — not market volatility
3. Liquidity equals dignity
4. Compounding needs time, not brilliance
5. Real estate needs balance, not obsession
6. Transparency beats promises — always
7. A good advisor is a force multiplier, not a cost

And the mental rewiring that makes these beliefs operational:

- From "safety" → real return
- From tangible → transparent and liquid

- From one-time decisions → lifelong habits
- From asset value → cash flow and exit clarity
- From DIY → advisor-guided structure

Just as patients shouldn't self-diagnose complex illnesses, doctors shouldn't self-manage complex wealth alone.

8.8 — Four Doctors, Four Biases

Dr. Sameer — Cardiac Surgeon, Hyderabad

Avoided equity after witnessing a market fall early in his career. Stayed FD and property-heavy for over a decade. Over 12 years he lost nearly ₹2 crore in opportunity cost despite making no "wrong" decisions — only safe ones. Loss aversion disguises itself as prudence.

Dr. Desai — General Surgeon, Navi Mumbai

Measured success through peer comparison and upgraded home and car early to match his circle. High EMIs crushed liquidity when elective surgeries slowed during Covid. Social proof turns lifestyle into a liability.

Both made decisions that felt rational in the moment. Both paid a compounding cost for it.

Dr. Priyanka — Oncologist, Coimbatore

Believed real estate never fails and focused only on positive stories while ignoring liquidity and exit realities. During a family emergency, she had assets — but no usable cash. Confirmation bias makes bad decisions feel repeatedly validated.

Dr. Gayatri — Endocrinologist, Vizag

Was anxious about markets and relied on peer advice instead of a plan. Shifted to an advisor-led structure with automation and asset allocation discipline. Built a ₹1.8 crore portfolio in 9 years on a moderate income. Process-led investing beats emotion-led investing over time.

One let emotion decide. The other one built a system that removed emotion from the equation.

8.9 — Are You Letting Psychology Limit Your Wealth?

Your financial psychology may be working against you if:

1. You avoid equity due to fear of short-term falls
2. You invest without understanding the exit
3. You feel anxious watching market movements
4. You overtrust builder assurances and peer recommendations
5. You mirror what successful colleagues are doing without analysis
6. You dislike small losses more than you value large gains
7. You have been delaying investing for more than a year
8. You hesitate to ask a qualified advisor for help

Three or more apply? Psychology — not income, not market conditions — is the primary constraint on your wealth.

Psychology, not income, decides whether money compounds or leaks.

Chapter 9

Family Pressures & Social Expectations

9.1 — The Decisions Doctors Never Make Alone

Indian doctors never make financial decisions in isolation. They decide amidst family opinions, peer advice, social expectations, cultural traditions, and constant comparison.

In India, money represents more than utility — it signals status, honour, family reputation, and identity. Doctors sit at the centre of this pressure. As a result, **more wealth is lost to family-driven decisions than to market volatility.** This chapter dissects those pressures — and shows how doctors can protect wealth without damaging relationships.

9.2 — The Cultural Reality: A Doctor Is a Family Asset

In most Indian families, a doctor is perceived as the most educated, responsible, stable, high-earning member — and the default financial decision-maker.

The assumption is unspoken but universal: you will help financially, you will "know" investments, you will buy property early, upgrade lifestyle quickly, and support relatives during crises. The pressure is rarely articulated. It is simply felt — every time a family gathering turns to money.

9.3 — Five Ways Family Pressure Shapes Financial Decisions

1. **Pressure to buy a home early** — Parents associate a home with stability and respect. Young doctors are rushed into overpriced properties, long EMIs, and early cash-flow stress before the financial foundation is ready.

2. **Pressure to buy property in the native place** — "Land is always safe." "At least one property in the hometown." The outcomes: illiquid assets, low XIRR, legal complexity, and emotional attachment without returns.

3. **Pressure to support extended family** — Doctors quietly become emergency financiers and fallback options for siblings, cousins, and extended relatives. Liquidity and compounding bear the cost.

4. **Pressure to upgrade lifestyle** — Premium cars, elite schools, better localities, generous hosting — each expected, each accelerating lifestyle creep before wealth is built.

5. **Pressure to invest like others** — Land syndicates, builder schemes, unlisted shares, agricultural plots — family approval replaces financial logic. The source of the idea is trusted. The idea itself is not examined.

9.4 — In-Law Influence: The Hidden Variable

Marriage merges two financial cultures. In-laws may carry strong opinions about money — jewellery-heavy allocations, ceremony-driven expenses, early home purchases, and decisions based on anecdote rather than analysis.

These preferences are often deeply held and rarely challenged. Unaddressed, they become a long-term friction point between what the couple needs financially and what the family expects socially.

9.5 — The Shame Factor: Why Doctors Don't Say No

Doctors struggle to refuse family and social pressure due to guilt, obligation, fear of judgment, and the weight of professional image. Even when timing is poor or liquidity is compromised, they comply — silently, repeatedly.

The emotional logic is clear: refusing feels selfish. Helping feels like the right thing to do. But **emotion-driven compliance erodes financial stability in ways that never fully recover.** The family gets helped today. The doctor's retirement gets quietly delayed.

9.6 — The Social Proof Trap Inside Medical Circles

Each specialty develops its own financial herd behaviour. Orthopaedic surgeons buy land. Radiologists buy clinics. Dermatologists upgrade cars. Dentists invest heavily in equipment. Doctors confuse peer behaviour with financial wisdom.

The same dynamic plays out in digital spaces. Alumni groups, hospital networks, specialty associations, and conference circles circulate property deals, stock tips, tax hacks, crypto noise, and "guaranteed" schemes freely. Because the source is a doctor, credibility is assumed.

> **Medical expertise does not translate into asset allocation skill.** Popularity does not equal prudence. A good idea from the wrong source is still a risk.

9.7 — Unchecked Obligation: The Quiet Wealth Destroyer

Doctors carry obligations to parents, spouse, children, and extended relatives — all valid, all real, all emotionally weighted. But obligation without structure is not generosity. It is depletion.

Unchecked obligation exhausts wealth before it secures the future. The doctor who helps everyone else first often reaches 55 with depleted liquidity, stalled compounding, and a retirement that depends on income continuing indefinitely.

9.8 — Five Boundaries Every Doctor Must Hold

1. **Immediate family first** — Parents matter deeply. But spouse and children come first in financial planning. Their security cannot be deferred for extended family obligations.
2. **Liquidity is sacred** — Never compromise emergency funds or automated SIPs for an emotional request. Once broken, the habit is hard to rebuild.
3. **No loans without structure** — Gift only what you can afford to lose. Avoid informal family lending — it damages both money and relationships when it goes wrong.
4. **No investment under pressure** — You don't treat a patient because they insist on a particular drug. Apply the same standard to financial decisions.
5. **Joint consent for major decisions** — Homes, land, cars, jewellery, and business investments must be jointly agreed with spouse. Shared decisions reduce risk — and future blame.

9.9 — The One Financial Sentence Every Doctor Must Learn

> **"I'll check with my financial plan and advisor, and get back to you."**
>
> This single sentence buys time, removes urgency, shifts emotion to logic, signals that a structure exists, and blocks manipulation — all without refusing, arguing, or offending.

9.10 — Four Doctors, Four Patterns

Dr. Anjali — Gynaecologist, Kanpur

Family pushed her to buy land for her daughter's future. It stayed illiquid for 12 years while investing stalled. Shifting surplus into REITs and hybrid funds eventually restored cash-flow visibility — but a decade of compounding was already lost. Emotionally right decisions can still be financially costly.

Dr. Kaveri — ENT Surgeon, Mangalore

In-laws pushed for a luxury villa to match professional status. EMIs crossed 45% of income and SIPs were cut entirely. Years of restructuring were needed to regain stability. Prestige housing silently kills compounding.

Both made decisions driven by family expectation rather than financial logic. Both paid for it in compounding years.

Dr. Rishi — Prosthodontist, Indore

An elder sibling convinced him to join a family investment in unlisted shares. Trust replaced due diligence. Capital stayed locked and was later written down significantly. Family trust is not a substitute for governance or exit clarity.

Dr. Suresh — Intensivist, Kurnool

Routed every major financial decision through a written plan and advisor review. By 40, his net worth exceeded peers nearly a decade senior. Boundaries — not income — decided the outcome.

One let family relationships bypass financial discipline while the other used a plan to separate emotion from decision.

9.11 — Social Success Without Financial Stress

1. **Choose identity over image** — Wealth is liquidity, freedom, and choice — not cars or houses. Define success by your net worth trajectory, not your visible standard of living.
2. **Explain, don't argue** — "We follow a financial plan" ends most debates without creating conflict.
3. **Reduce disclosure** — Fewer people knowing your financial position means fewer opinions, fewer requests, and safer decisions.
4. **Use your advisor as a buffer** — When pressured, blame the plan or the advisor — not yourself. "My advisor said we can't do this right now" is a complete and sufficient answer.
5. **Build a strong spouse alliance** — A united doctor-couple with shared financial goals is the most effective defence against external pressure. Shared decisions reduce both risk and future blame.

9.12 — Before You Move On

In the last two years, how many financial decisions have been influenced by family expectation, peer comparison, or social obligation rather than your financial plan?

Family matters. Society influences. Culture is powerful. But your financial life cannot run on guilt, comparison, or obligation. It must run on clarity, planning, and boundaries.

When you protect your financial life, you protect your family better than any cheque ever could.

Chapter 10

Cash Flow Mastery

Clinic + Personal

10.1 — Why Cash Flow Matters More Than Income

Most doctors chase higher income — more consultations, more surgeries, more shifts. But wealth is not built by how much you earn. It is built by how much you keep, how predictably it flows, and how deliberately it is directed.

> **Cash flow is the bloodstream of your financial life.** Just as poor circulation damages organs silently, poor cash flow corrodes financial health quietly — until a crisis makes it visible.

10.2 — Why Doctors Face Complex Cash Flow Challenges

1. **Inconsistent income** — OPD volumes, surgical loads, and diagnostic revenue fluctuate with seasons, hospital politics, and referral patterns
2. **Dual expense streams** — clinic costs and personal costs both run simultaneously and neither pauses when income dips
3. **Multiple dependents** — parents, in-laws, siblings, spouse, and children all carry legitimate financial claims
4. **Unplanned costs** — equipment repairs, legal issues, and family health crises arrive without warning

5. **Early underpricing** — low initial consultation rates distort income expectations for years
6. **Fatigue-driven decisions** — burnout reduces clinical throughput and pushes doctors toward convenience spending

Cash flow stays fragile until it is systematised.

10.3 — The Doctor's Cash Flow Pyramid

- **Level 1 — Clinic Essentials** — rent, staff salaries, consumables, equipment, utilities, compliance
- **Level 2 — Personal Essentials** — home rent or EMI, groceries, children's expenses, health insurance
- **Level 3 — Growth Investments** — SIPs, STPs, REITs, hybrid funds, PMS/AIF commitments
- **Level 4 — Professional Growth** — courses, conferences, equipment upgrades, clinic improvements
- **Level 5 — Lifestyle Upgrades** — vacations, gadgets, luxury, celebrations

Most doctors mistakenly treat Level 5 as Level 2 — reversing priorities and destabilising cash flow permanently.

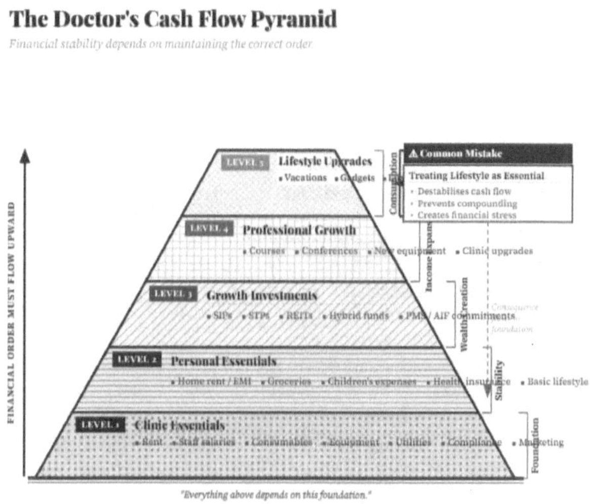

Figure 10.3 — Financial stability requires maintaining the correct order. Reversing priorities destabilises long-term wealth creation.

10.4 — The One Golden Rule: Invest First. Spend After.

Most doctors follow: Personal → Clinic → Lifestyle → Investments (if anything remains). Reverse the sequence:

1. **10–15% → Emergency fund** — non-negotiable, automated
2. **Automate SIPs and STPs** — before anything else moves
3. **Insurance premiums + essentials** — fixed, non-discretionary
4. **Clinic operations** — staff and running costs
5. **Professional growth** — courses, equipment upgrades
6. **Lifestyle** — last, from what remains

The money does not change. The order does.

10.5 — The Six-Account System

Doctors should operate six dedicated bank accounts, not two. Segregation prevents mixing, leakage, and emotional withdrawals.

1. **Clinic Income Account** — all professional receipts flow here first
2. **Clinic Operations Account** — rent, staff salaries, consumables, maintenance
3. **Clinic Growth Account** — equipment upgrades, training, digital marketing
4. **Household Expense Account** — family spending and utilities
5. **Investment Account** — all SIPs, REITs, hybrid funds, PMS/AIF routed here
6. **Emergency & Stability Fund** — 9–12 months of combined expenses

10.6 — Surplus Benchmarks by Career Stage

- Residents: 5–10% of income
- Early career (3–7 years): 15–25%
- Mid-career (7–15 years): 25–35%
- Established (15+ years): 30–40%
- Doctor couples: 35–50%

If you are below benchmark for your stage, lifestyle is outrunning cash flow.

10.7 — EMI Overload: The Cash Flow Killer

Home, clinic, car, equipment, personal loan, education loan, credit card rollover, renovation loan — EMIs accumulate in ways that feel individually manageable and collectively suffocating.

> When total EMIs exceed 35% of monthly income, financial stress compounds. The ceiling: **EMIs ≤ 30% of net income.**

10.8 — How to Stabilise Income Flow

- Diversify income sources: OPD, surgeries, diagnostics, teaching, tele-consultations
- Plan for seasonality: structure SIP step-ups around cyclical income peaks
- Avoid single-hospital dependence: diversify practice locations
- Negotiate minimum guaranteed retainers: combine fixed and variable for predictability

10.9 — The 40–20–20–20 Personal Cash Flow Model

- **40% — Personal essentials** — home, food, insurance, school fees
- **20% — Clinic contribution** — if running private practice
- **20% — Wealth investments** — SIPs, REITs, hybrid funds, PMS/AIF
- **20% — Lifestyle and flexibility** — travel, celebrations, upgrades

The investment floor of 20% is non-negotiable. The lifestyle ceiling of 20% is the discipline that protects it.

10.10 — If You Have the Cash, Should You Still Take a Home Loan?

A doctor plans to buy a ₹2 crore house. The full amount is available. Income is stable and can comfortably service an EMI. The question is not affordability — it is whether the ₹2 crore should be deployed on the house or kept invested while taking a loan.

A concept widely circulating on social media: take a ₹2 crore home loan at 7.5%, invest the corpus in mutual funds, and use an SWP to pay the EMI. This is theoretically attractive but assumes stable, predictable returns. If markets fall in early years while withdrawals continue, capital erodes. This hidden vulnerability is called **sequence risk.** The decision must be evaluated structurally, not emotionally.

Assumptions: *₹2 crore house · 7.5% loan · 10-year tenure · EMI ₹2.37L/month · Hybrid fund 9% CAGR · Equity fund 14% CAGR*

Option 1 — Pay Cash, Then Invest Monthly (Dr. Anitha)

Buys outright with ₹2 crore. Invests ₹2.37 lakh/month from income into equity at 14% CAGR.

After 10 years: Total SIP: ₹2.85 crore → Portfolio: ₹6.22 crore. Consistent investing allows compounding to work at full strength.

Option 2 — Loan + Invest Corpus via STP (Dr. Ramesh)

Takes loan. Invests ₹2 crore in hybrid fund at 9% CAGR. Transfers ₹1.67L/month via STP to equity. Pays ₹2.37L EMI from income.

After 10 years: Hybrid: ₹1.68 crore + STP equity: ₹4.32 crore = ₹6.00 crore. Capital invested early gives compounding a head start.

Option 3 — Loan + Equity + SWP (Dr. Sunil)

Takes loan. Invests ₹2 crore fully in equity. Withdraws ₹2.37L/month via SWP to pay EMI.

After 10 years: Portfolio remaining: ₹1.89 crore. Despite 26.3% XIRR label, most gains are consumed by withdrawals. Lowest actual wealth of the three options.

Decision Matrix — Same House, Three Different Financial Outcomes

	Option 1 Pay Cash + SIP	**Option 2 Loan + Hybrid → STP**	**Option 3 Loan + Equity + SWP**
House purchase	Cash outright	Loan	Loan
Initial cash deployed	₹2.00 crore	₹0	₹0
Monthly commitment	₹2.37L SIP (from income)	₹2.37L EMI (from income)	EMI funded from portfolio
Investment strategy	Monthly SIP into equity fund	₹2Cr in hybrid + STP to equity	₹2Cr in equity, SWP for EMI
Portfolio value after 10 years	**₹6.22 crore**	**₹6.00 crore**	**₹1.89 crore**
XIRR	12.9%	14.5%	26.3% (misleading)
Compounding interruption	None	Low (EMI from income)	High (SWP drains fund)
Wealth creation	★★★★★ **Highest**	★★★★ **High**	★★ **Moderate**

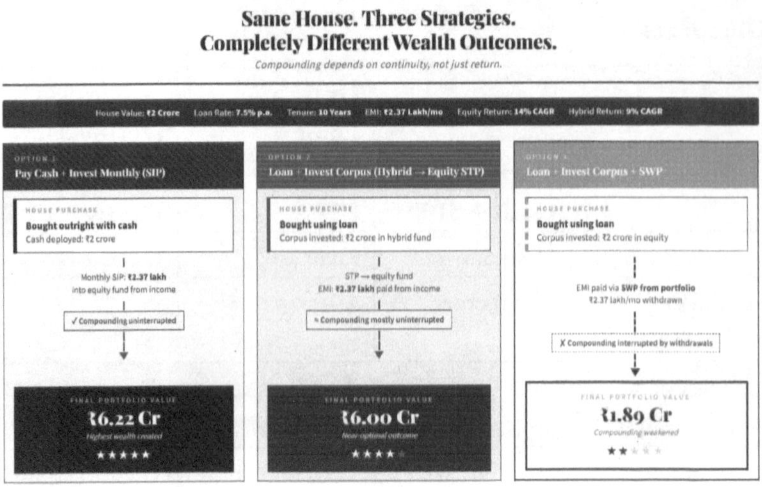

Figure 10.10 — Wealth outcomes depend on how long capital remains uninterrupted. Frequent withdrawals weaken compounding, even at high returns.

House Value: ₹2 crore | Loan: 7.5% | Tenure: 10 years | EMI: ₹2.37 lakh/month

Note: Returns assumed. Tax implications and inflation not factored.

Same house. Same returns. Completely different wealth outcomes.

Option 1 (pay cash + SIP): highest long-term wealth.

Option 2 (loan + corpus): nearly similar wealth with better capital efficiency.

Option 3 (SWP for EMI): highest XIRR label, lowest actual wealth.

Wealth is determined not just by return — but by time and continuity.

10.11 — The Medical Equipment Lifecycle Fund

Dr. Priyanka — Gynaecologist, Hyderabad

Dr. Priyanka runs her own ob-gyn clinic in Hyderabad. She is ready to buy a mid-range HD obstetric ultrasound quoted at ₹25 lakh. The equipment salesman has offered three options: cash purchase, bank loan, or manufacturer lease. Each sounds reasonable. What nobody has told her is that the financing decision and the replacement decision are the same decision — she just doesn't know it yet.

Step 1 — Three Ways to Buy the Machine (Years 0–5)

	Cash Purchase	**Bank / NBFC Loan**	**Manufacturer Lease**
Upfront outflow	₹25.0 lakh	Nil	Nil
Monthly commitment	Nil	₹51,291 / month	₹53,000 / month
Total outflow (5 yrs)	₹25.0 lakh	₹30.8 lakh	₹31.8 lakh
Depreciation tax shield	₹7.42 lakh	₹7.42 lakh	Not applicable
Interest / lease tax saving	—	₹1.73 lakh	₹9.54 lakh
Net true cost after tax	**₹17.6 lakh**	**₹21.6 lakh**	**₹22.3 lakh**
Asset owned at end	Yes	Yes	No
Break-even scans / day	2.7	3.3	3.4

Break-even check: Dr. Priyanka does 10 scans/day on average. All three break-evens (2.7 to 3.4 scans/day) are comfortably within even her slowest week. The machine pays for itself under any financing option.

Note on manufacturer leasing: the net cost of ₹22.3 lakh vs ₹17.6 lakh for cash is a difference of ₹4.7 lakh over five years, and no asset is owned at the end. If an AMC is bundled, verify it independently — standalone AMC costs approximately ₹1.6 lakh/year.

Step 2 — The Inflation Insight

At 8% annual equipment inflation, the replacement machine at Year 5 costs ₹36.7 lakh. Scan fees also inflate at 8% — from ₹600 to ₹882 per scan.

> **Key insight:** when equipment cost and scan fees both inflate at 8%, the break-even scan volume at Year 5 is identical to Year 0. The upgrade treadmill does not get harder in relative terms — only in absolute numbers.

Step 3 — The Medical Equipment Lifecycle Fund

Purpose: to build a dedicated corpus over 5 years that funds the replacement machine at Year 5, without disrupting clinical income or existing investments.

Deriving the target: the current machine costs ₹25 lakh. At 8% annual equipment inflation, the replacement costs ₹36.7 lakh in 5 years. That is the savings target.

Why an 8% step-up SIP? The SIP steps up at the same rate as equipment inflation — so the savings rate keeps exact pace with the rising cost. A flat SIP falls behind; a 8% step-up SIP stays aligned.

Year 1: ₹40,000/month *starting SIP*

Year 2: ₹43,200/month *+8% step-up*

Year 3: ₹46,656/month *+8% step-up*

Year 4: ₹50,388/month *+8% step-up*

Year 5: ₹54,420/month *+8% step-up*

Pre-tax corpus at Year 5: ₹38.01 lakh

Capital gains tax: SIP investments from Month 1 to Month 48 (held >12 months) attract LTCG at 12.5% on gains above ₹1 lakh. SIP investments from Month 49 to Month 60 (held ≤12 months) attract STCG at 20%. Total tax: ₹1.14 lakh.

Post-tax corpus: ₹36.9 lakh — covers the replacement machine of ₹36.7 lakh with a small buffer. ✓

Total invested: Monthly SIPs of ₹40,000, ₹43,200, ₹46,656, ₹50,388 & ₹54,420 in each year respectively = ₹28.16 lakh over 60 months

The EMI Transition (Loan Option)

Under the loan option, when the EMI of ₹51,291/month ends at Month 60, the freed amount comfortably covers the Year 6 Lifecycle SIP of ₹58,773/month (the next step-up in the series), with a ₹7,482/month surplus from income growth. The discipline already exists — it simply redirects.

Step 4 — Three Replacement Options at Year 5

At the end of Year 5, Dr. Priyanka has a post-tax corpus of approximately ₹36.9 lakh in her Lifecycle Fund. The replacement machine costs ₹36.7 lakh. Three paths forward, each with a different approach to Years 6–10:

Option A — Full Deployment: use the entire ₹36.9L post-tax corpus to buy machine outright. Zero debt. Machine owned immediately. The Lifecycle SIP then **continues from Year 6** at ₹58,773/month (next step-up), building ₹54.1L post-tax by Year 10 — just covering the ₹53.9L Year 10 replacement. The cycle is self-perpetuating.

Option B — Partial Payment + Loan: put ₹22L down, take a ₹14.7L loan. The logic: borrow at 8.5% while the residual ₹14.9L stays invested at 12% — the positive spread justifies the loan. EMI: ₹30,159/month (only 13% of Year 5 income). **Lifecycle SIP also continues from Year 6** at ₹58,773/month. Residual grows to ₹24.9L post-tax by Year 10.

Option C — Keep Corpus Intact: take a fresh loan for the full ₹36.7L and leave the entire corpus compounding. EMI: ₹75,296/month — which is 33% of Year 5 income. Crucially, this is the **same percentage** as the original EMI was of Year 0 income — the burden is identical relative to income. **No separate Lifecycle SIP is needed** — the corpus itself grows to ₹61.6L by Year 10 and funds the next replacement directly.

	Option A Full Deployment	Option B Partial + Loan	Option C Corpus Intact
Post-tax corpus at Y5	**₹36.9L**	**₹36.9L**	**₹36.9L**
Down payment	₹36.9L (full)	₹22L	Nil
Loan taken	Nil	₹14.7L	₹36.7L
EMI (Years 6–10)	Nil	**₹30,159/month (13% of Y5 income)**	**₹75,296/ month (33% of Y5 income)**
Lifecycle SIP (Years 6–10)	Continues: ₹58,773 start, 8% step-up	Continues: ₹58,773 start, 8% step-up	Not needed — corpus funds next replacement
Corpus / wealth at Year 10 (post-tax)	SIP builds ₹54.1L for Y10 machine (₹53.9L) ✓	**Residual: ₹24.9L + SIP: ₹54.1L**	**₹61.6L (see note below)**
Verdict	Self-sustaining cycle. Clean.	Capital-efficient. Positive spread.	**Maximum wealth. 33% EMI = same as original Y0 burden.**

** Under Option C, if the corpus is not sold at Year 5 (i.e., no tax event occurs), it continues compounding from the pre-tax value of ₹37.94 lakh, growing to approximately ₹63.5 lakh post-tax by Year 10 — higher than shown.*

The Option C insight: the doctor who runs the Lifecycle SIP and chooses Option C has converted 5 years of equipment finance discipline into a **₹61–63 lakh permanent wealth corpus** by Year 10 — without ever intending to become an investor.

Figure 10.11b — The Medical Equipment Lifecycle Fund: Year 0 purchase → Years 1–5 step-up Lifecycle SIP + post-tax corpus → Year 5 fork into Options A, B, or C → Year 10 outcomes and Lifecycle SIP continuity.

Before buying any piece of equipment, answer two questions:

Which financing option fits my current cash flow and corpus position?

Have I started the Lifecycle SIP from Day 1 at ₹40,000/month with 8% annual step-up — so the next replacement is already funded before I need it?

Equipment replacement is not a future problem. It is a present decision, made on the day you buy the machine.

10.12 — Before You Move On

Two questions for your current cash flow:

Does investing happen automatically before you decide how to spend the rest — or does it happen with whatever remains after spending?

Do your total EMIs stay below 30% of monthly income — or have commitments quietly accumulated beyond that threshold?

If either answer is uncomfortable, the six-account system and the invest-first sequence are the structural fixes. Both can be implemented within a month.

Chapter 11

Emergency Fund & Financial Safety Nets

11.1 — The One Safety Net Every Doctor Needs First

If there is one element that prevents a doctor's financial life from collapsing during a crisis, it is not income, not investments, and certainly not property. It is **liquidity.**

Doctors face sudden financial shocks more often than almost any other profession — abrupt staff attrition, temporary clinic shutdowns, medico-legal notices, equipment failure, and family medical emergencies.

> *"An emergency fund is the oxygen cylinder of your financial life. You may not use it daily — but when you need it, the absence is catastrophic."*

This chapter explains how to build a robust, layered financial safety net that protects income, investments, and peace of mind.

11.2 — Why Doctors Need a Larger Emergency Fund

Doctors require deeper buffers than most professionals for five specific reasons:

1. **Income is inherently unpredictable** — unlike salaried professionals, monthly earnings fluctuate with OPD volumes, surgical loads, and hospital payment cycles
2. **Multiple people depend on one engine** — parents, spouse, children, and clinic staff all rely on the continuity of one income source

3. **Medical emergencies cost more for doctors** — doctors rarely choose basic care — they choose faster intervention, premium hospitals, and advanced diagnostics. Costs escalate rapidly.

4. **Professional emergencies are unique** — clinic breakdowns, equipment failures, and legal notices can trigger zero income plus immediate expenses simultaneously

5. **Doctors rarely stop working by choice** — when forced to pause, income often drops to zero immediately with no severance, no notice period, no buffer from an employer

11.3 — The Doctor Emergency Fund Formula

- **Absolute minimum** — 6 months of combined household + clinic expenses
- **Recommended (most doctors)** — 9–12 months
- **Optimal (high-risk specialties)** — 12–18 months — surgeons, radiologists, anaesthetists, self-employed specialists

If your emergency fund is below 6 months: stress rises, EMIs become dangerous, SIPs get paused, and lifestyle destabilises. *Think of an emergency fund as a financial stabilising hormone.*

11.4 — Where to Keep the Emergency Fund

The objective is liquidity, safety, and immediate access — not returns. Four suitable options, in order of preference:

- **Liquid mutual funds (most recommended)** — T+1 liquidity, ~5–7% returns, SEBI-regulated, no lock-in. Best for most doctors.
- **Overnight funds** — negligible volatility, highest safety among mutual funds. Best for ultra-conservative doctors.
- **High-interest savings accounts** — instant access, easy to operate. Returns are lower but accessibility is maximum.
- **Sweep FD accounts** — partial FD breakup with instant access. Useful for clinics managing operational cash. Taxed at slab rate.

11.5 — Where an Emergency Fund Must Never Be Kept

Emergency money must never be parked in:

- Locked FDs or long-duration debt funds
- Real estate, land, or physical gold jewellery
- ULIPs, endowment plans, or money-back policies
- PMS, AIF, SIF, or unlisted shares
- Crypto assets or speculative instruments

Emergency funds must be safe, liquid, and predictable. Not illiquid, volatile, or speculative. Every rupee of emergency fund in the wrong instrument is a rupee unavailable when it matters most.

11.6 — Building the Fund: Monthly Contribution

Emergency fund creation comes before all investing. The fund must be complete before SIPs are treated as the primary financial priority.

Example: Required fund ₹10 lakh · Existing ₹2 lakh · Gap ₹8 lakh · Saving ₹50,000/month → **16 months to target**

Accelerate using bonuses, incentives, tax refunds, and consultation windfalls. Compressing this timeline increases confidence immediately and frees the mental bandwidth needed for longer-term investing.

11.7 — The 3-Bucket Safety Net Model

- **Bucket 1 — Emergency Fund (Liquidity)** — 6–12 months of expenses in liquid or overnight funds. Immediate access. No exceptions.
- **Bucket 2 — Contingency Cushion (Protection)** — term insurance, health insurance, personal accident cover, and professional indemnity. Transfers catastrophic risk off the balance sheet.
- **Bucket 3 — Stability Buffer (Flexibility)** — short-term debt or arbitrage funds for clinic repairs, staff settlements, and legal expenses that are foreseeable but not immediate.

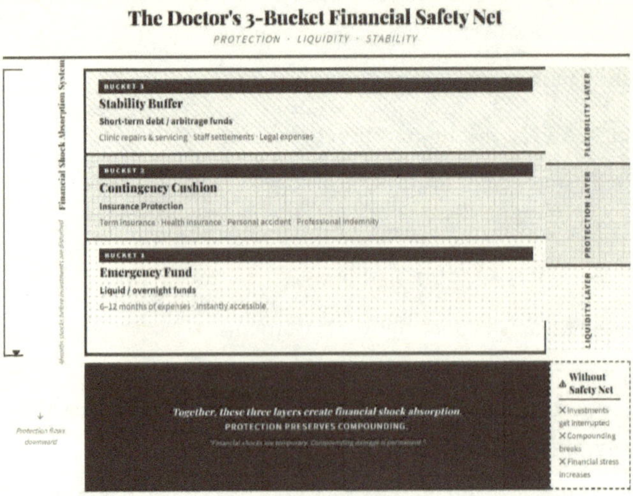

Figure 11.7 — The three buckets absorb financial shocks at different levels and protect long-term investments from interruption. Compounding succeeds not because markets are stable, but because investors are protected.

11.8 — Five Essential Insurances for Doctors

1. **Term insurance** — 15–20× annual income. Protects family independence if income stops permanently.

2. **Health insurance** — individual base + family floater of ₹1 crore recommended, with super top-up. Doctors choose premium care — cover must match that reality.

3. **Personal accident insurance** — protects against disability that stops income without death. Often overlooked, rarely optional.

4. **Professional indemnity insurance** — mandatory for all practising doctors. Covers legal fees and settlement costs from medico-legal complaints.

5. **Clinic and equipment insurance** — fire, theft, and breakdown cover. Equipment failure without insurance means personal funds absorb the loss.

Insurance is not an investment. It is a safety net. The two must never be mixed.

11.9 — Common Safety Net Mistakes

- Depending only on spouse income as the backup plan
- Using credit cards as emergency funds — expensive and limits compounding
- Treating locked FDs as liquidity buffers
- Mixing clinic and household emergency reserves in one account
- Letting lifestyle upgrades quietly erode the emergency corpus
- Relying on "future income will cover it" — future income is not yet earned
- Mistaking insurance policy surrender value for liquid emergency money

These mistakes surface only during crisis — when correction is hardest and the cost is highest.

11.10 — Four Doctors, Four Safety Net Lessons

Dr. Mohan — Urologist, Hyderabad

A short circuit caused a fire in his clinic, shutting operations for weeks. With clinic insurance and a 9-month emergency fund, he managed salaries, rent, and family expenses without a single loan. The disruption stayed operational — not financial.

Dr. Karthik — Dermatologist, Vellore

A sudden family medical emergency needed immediate hospitalisation and travel. He redeemed from a liquid fund within a day instead of breaking equity investments or borrowing from colleagues. Compounding continued without disruption.

Insurance absorbed the damage. Liquidity absorbed the shock. Both outcomes depended on preparation, not income.

Dr. Preethi — Endodontist, Berhampur

During Covid, her clinic stayed shut for months and income dropped sharply. She used her emergency buffer to run the household, retain key staff, and restart smoothly. She avoided loans and regained momentum faster than peers. Emergency funds buy time — and dignity — when income disappears.

Dr. Kavitha — Intensivist, Tirupati

A professional complaint escalated into legal proceedings. Her professional indemnity insurance covered legal fees and settlement costs entirely. A legal crisis did not become financial burnout. Some risks are non-negotiable — they must be insured.

Both faced crises outside their control. Both had structured protection in place before the crisis arrived.

11.11 — Emergency Readiness Check

Six questions. Any "No" signals active vulnerability:

1. Do I have 9–12 months of combined household and clinic expenses saved in a liquid fund?
2. Can I absorb a ₹5–10 lakh clinic shock without a loan?
3. Can I handle immediate legal expenses without selling investments?
4. Is professional indemnity insurance active and adequate for my specialty?
5. Is my family protected with term insurance of at least 15–20× annual income?
6. Will my household run for 12 months if income stops entirely?

Any "No" answer is not a future problem. It is a present vulnerability that the next chapter builds toward addressing.

Chapter 12

Doctor-Specific Risk Management

12.1 — Why Doctors Face Unique Financial Risks

Every profession carries risk. But doctors operate in a high-risk convergence zone — where financial, legal, medical, emotional, and reputational risks overlap and amplify each other.

A doctor's risk profile is shaped by volatile and irregular income, rising patient expectations, expanding medico-legal scrutiny, capital-intensive clinics, dependence on personal health and stamina, and multi-generational responsibilities.

> **Risk management is not a defensive add-on.** It is core survival infrastructure. This chapter provides a 360-degree framework to identify, prioritise, and protect against every major risk a doctor faces — systematically, not emotionally.

12.2 — Five Major Risk Zones

- **Risk Zone 1 — Personal** — premature death, disability, serious illness, accidents
- **Risk Zone 2 — Professional** — negligence cases, patient complaints, regulatory scrutiny, reputational damage
- **Risk Zone 3 — Practice** — clinic fire, equipment failure, theft, staff fraud

- **Risk Zone 4 — Financial** — unsuitable investments, excessive EMIs, weak cash-flow structure, market corrections without buffers
- **Risk Zone 5 — Family** — parents' health emergencies, children's education cost spikes, unexpected obligations

Ignoring even one zone can trigger cascading failure across the others.

12.3 — Risk 1: Mortality — Term Insurance

The precise question every doctor must answer: *"If my income stops tomorrow, does my family inherit freedom — or financial fragility?"*

A doctor's greatest asset is future earning capacity. When that stops prematurely, the loss is not one year's income — it is decades of compounding that never happens. The formula for adequate cover:

> **Term Cover = Annual Income × Remaining Working Years**
>
> Example: Income ₹30 lakh, 20 years remaining → Cover **₹6 crore**

For most doctors, 15–20× annual income is the practical baseline. Term insurance is cheapest when taken early — before lifestyle conditions narrow insurability. Review and enhance cover every 4–5 years as income grows.

> **Your portfolio compounds wealth. Your income makes that compounding possible. Term insurance protects the source.**
>
> *Wealth creation begins not with return — but with protection.*

12.4 — Risk 2: Disability — Personal Accident Insurance

Doctors depend disproportionately on hands, eyesight, and fine motor control. An accident causing temporary or permanent, partial or total disability can stop income overnight.

Personal accident insurance covers disability income replacement and accidental death. Recommended cover: ₹50 lakh – ₹1 crore depending on specialty. This is one of the most underestimated doctor risks — and one of the simplest to insure.

12.5 — Risk 3: Health — Health Insurance + Top-Ups

Doctors understand healthcare costs better than anyone — yet remain chronically underinsured. They choose premium hospitals, higher room categories, and advanced diagnostics. Cover must match that reality.

- **Base cover** — ₹50 lakh individual or floater with a super top-up of ₹25–100 lakh
- **Include** — parents if dependent, day-care treatments, maternity where relevant

This structure ensures medical events never force liquidation of investments or interruption of SIPs.

12.6 — Risk 4: Medico-Legal Exposure — Professional Indemnity

Medico-legal risk is now inseparable from medical practice. Rising patient awareness, social media, and aggressive legal systems mean even competent doctors face litigation. Skill and intent offer no immunity.

A single complaint can trigger legal action, reputational damage, emotional strain, and heavy financial costs. Hospitals do not always protect individual doctors. This risk is not about *if* — it is about *when.* The correct protection structure and coverage benchmarks are detailed in **Chapter 13.**

12.7 — Risk 5: Clinic, Equipment, and Practice Interruption

Your clinic is not just a workplace. It is your primary income engine. Two categories of protection are essential:

- **Clinic and equipment cover** — fire insurance, equipment breakdown, theft, and staff fraud. Small annual premiums protect assets worth crores.

- **Practice interruption cover** — if the clinic shuts due to fire, equipment damage, structural repairs, or landlord disputes, income stops while fixed costs continue. Business interruption cover — or a robust emergency fund — prevents financial paralysis.

12.8 — Risk 6: Real Estate Overexposure

When 60–80% of net worth sits in property, any slowdown in that asset class is not a portfolio problem — it is a personal financial crisis. Poor liquidity, unpredictable exits, and mounting maintenance costs expose the structural fragility that was invisible during the accumulation phase. *Chapter 5 works through this in full detail.*

Safe allocation: real estate ≤ 25–30% of total net worth, including the primary home.

12.9 — Risk 7: Investment Traps

Builder-linked schemes, dubious PMS structures, high-commission ULIPs, crypto hype, and unrelated business partnerships are recurring traps for doctors. The protection is always the same: XIRR, exit clarity, regulation, and liquidity. *Chapter 3 covers the nine myths that lead into these traps.*

12.10 — Risk 8: EMI Overload

When total EMIs exceed 30–35% of monthly income, liquidity collapses, investments stall, and every income disruption becomes a crisis. The structural fix — the six-account system and the invest-first sequence — is covered in *Chapter 10*.

12.11 — The Risk Management Blueprint

A simple seven-step protocol that applies across every life stage:

1. **Identify** — map every risk zone annually — personal, professional, practice, financial, family
2. **Insure** — transfer non-manageable risks to insurance products
3. **Liquidity** — maintain 9–12 months of expenses in accessible funds at all times

4. **Diversify** — no single asset class beyond 30% of net worth except equity in accumulation phase
5. **Control leverage** — EMIs ≤ 30% of income, no loan under social pressure
6. **Avoid traps** — XIRR + exit clarity + regulation are the three filters
7. **Review annually** — risk profile changes as income, family, and practice evolve

12.12 — Four Doctors, Four Risk Lessons

Dr. Aravind — Neurosurgeon, Vijayawada

Skipped professional indemnity cover assuming experience was enough. A complication triggered legal notices and ₹7 lakh in legal costs. Stress affected clinical focus and reputation. Skill does not remove legal risk. Insurance protects when skill cannot.

Dr. Harish — Gastroenterologist, Mathura

A short circuit caused a clinic fire and damaged diagnostic equipment. Insurance reimbursed approximately ₹4 lakh. The clinic reopened quickly — no loans, no liquidation of investments. Small premiums protect large professional assets.

Both faced professional risks outside their control. One was protected. One was not.

Dr. Kamala — Cardiologist, Kolhapur

Built ₹1.5 crore across three properties with weak rental cash flow and poor liquidity. A slowdown in practice exposed the fragility. She rebuilt liquidity and shifted surplus into REITs and hybrid funds. Real estate without liquidity increases risk. Diversification restores control.

Dr. Aditi — Embryologist, Nagpur

A road accident caused temporary disability and she could not operate for four months. Personal accident cover ensured income replacement throughout. EMIs and household expenses were met without borrowing. Health insurance covers treatment. PA insurance protects income.

Both faced personal and financial risks. Structured protection meant neither became a financial crisis.

12.13 — Before You Move On

A quick risk audit — answer honestly:

Is term insurance in place at 15–20× annual income?

Is professional indemnity active and adequate for your specialty?

Is the clinic insured against fire, equipment failure, and theft?

Is personal accident cover in place for disability income replacement?

Does real estate stay within 25–30% of total net worth?

Do total EMIs stay below 30% of monthly income?

Risk management does not prevent problems. It prevents problems from destroying your financial life.

Chapter 13

Insurance Essentials for Doctors

13.1 — Insurance Is Not an Investment

Thousands of doctors lose crores over their careers by mixing insurance with investing — locking money into low-return, guaranteed policies that deliver poor protection and weaker returns.

> **Insurance exists for one purpose:** to transfer risks you cannot afford to handle yourself.
>
> **Insurance protects wealth. Investments create wealth.** Never mix the two.

13.2 — Four Golden Rules

1. **Insure only what can financially destroy you** — If a risk can wipe out your family's stability or your practice, insure it. If it cannot, do not.

2. **Pay the lowest premium for the highest protection** — Choose only pure covers: term, health, personal accident, professional indemnity, clinic and equipment insurance.

3. **Insurance + investment products are structurally flawed** — ULIPs, endowments, and money-back plans deliver poor returns, weak protection, and long lock-ins. Avoid completely.

4. **Insurance is your foundation, not your future** — Insurance ensures survival. Investments ensure growth. Confusing the two destroys both.

13.3 — The Six Essential Covers

Cover 1 — Term Insurance (Income Replacement)

Purpose: replace income if you are no longer alive to earn it. Formula: **Remaining working years × annual income**. At ₹30 lakh income with 20 years remaining, cover required is ₹6 crore. Practical baseline: 15–20× annual income. Buy before age 40 when premiums are lowest and underwriting is clean. Review every 4–5 years as income grows.

Assets are illiquid. Families need cash flow, not property.

Cover 2 — Health Insurance (Individual + Family Floater)

Doctors choose premium hospitals, higher room categories, and advanced diagnostics. Cover must match that reality. Recommended: base cover ₹50 lakh minimum with a super top-up of ₹50–100 lakh. Include spouse, children, and dependent parents. Super top-ups provide massive catastrophic protection at very low additional premium.

Cover 3 — Personal Accident Insurance

Doctors depend on hands, eyesight, and fine motor control. An accident causing temporary or permanent disability stops income immediately.

> **Death ends income permanently. Disability destroys income while you are alive.**
>
> Term insurance covers death. PA insurance protects your profession. Recommended cover: ₹50 lakh – ₹1 crore depending on specialty.

Cover 4 — Professional Indemnity Insurance

Mandatory in today's medico-legal environment. Rising patient awareness, social media, and aggressive legal systems mean even competent doctors face litigation. Skill and intent offer no immunity. A single complaint can trigger legal action, reputational damage, and financial costs that hospitals do not always absorb.

Indicative coverage benchmarks by specialty:

- Surgeons: ₹1–3 crore
- High-risk specialties (cardiac, neuro, obstetric): ₹2–5 crore
- Anaesthetists: ₹2–3 crore
- Radiologists: ₹1–2 crore
- Physicians and Paediatricians: ₹1–2 crore
- Dentists: ₹50 lakh – ₹1 crore

"I'm careful, nothing will happen." "My hospital will protect me." Insurance exists for the case you never expect.

Cover 5 — Clinic and Equipment Insurance

Your clinic is your primary income engine. If it stops, income stops. Essential covers: fire and short circuit, equipment breakdown, theft, and staff fraud. Small annual premiums protect assets worth crores and prevent cash-flow disruption that forces personal funds into the gap.

Cover 6 — Critical Illness Rider (Optional)

Provides a lump sum on diagnosis of cancer, stroke, or organ failure — covering income loss and non-medical expenses during recovery. **Only as a rider to health insurance — never as a stand-alone policy.** The stand-alone version is expensive, overlapping, and usually unnecessary if health insurance is adequately structured.

13.4 — Products Doctors Must Avoid

- ULIPs and guaranteed-return policies
- Endowment and money-back plans
- Traditional long-lock-in policies
- Child plans structured as insurance products

These products mix insurance and investment inefficiently. They deliver poor returns, weak protection, long lock-ins, and severely compromise the compounding years that matter most.

13.5 — The Insurance Checklist

- **Must-have** — term insurance, health insurance, personal accident cover, professional indemnity
- **Should-have** — health super top-up, clinic and equipment insurance
- **Optional** — critical illness rider (only as health insurance add-on)
- **Avoid completely** — ULIPs, endowments, traditional and guaranteed-return products

Common mistakes that undermine this checklist:

- Buying expensive policies early in career under agent pressure
- Using insurance primarily for tax saving under Section 80C
- Relying only on corporate health cover — which lapses when employment changes
- Ignoring personal accident and professional indemnity entirely
- Locking surplus into low-return policies for decades instead of investing

13.6 — Four Doctors, Four Insurance Lessons

Dr. Nikhil — Andrologist, Baroda

Took PA and professional indemnity early in his career. A road accident caused temporary disability; indemnity simultaneously handled legal issues from cancelled procedures. Income disruption stayed manageable. Disability risk often exceeds death risk for practising doctors.

Dr. Abhijit — Obstetrician, Asansol

Bought a ₹23 lakh ULIP at age 28. High premiums restricted SIPs and returns stayed weak. Compounding was delayed through the peak early-career years when it would have had the greatest impact. Mixing insurance and investing quietly destroys wealth.

One structured protection correctly from the start. One paid a decade-long compounding penalty for a single early mistake.

Dr. Kavya — Diabetologist, Vijayawada

Delayed her parents' health insurance. A sudden hospitalisation forced ₹8 lakh out-of-pocket and the liquidation of equity investments at an inopportune time. A preventable expense became a portfolio setback. Uninsured dependents are hidden liabilities.

Dr. Jaya — Ophthalmologist, Kannur

A clinic fire damaged equipment. Insurance funded replacements without a loan. Practice resumed quickly with minimal income loss. Business insurance protects continuity, not just assets.

Both faced unexpected events outside their control. Structured insurance meant neither became a financial crisis.

13.7 — Before You Move On

A quick insurance audit:

Is term insurance in place at 15–20× annual income?

Is health cover at least ₹50 lakh base with a super top-up?

Are parents covered under a separate health policy?

Is professional indemnity active and adequate for your specialty?

Is personal accident cover in place for disability income replacement?

Has any ULIP or endowment been allowed to persist beyond its surrender window?

The best investment returns come after protection is already in place.

Chapter 14

Legal & Compliance Checklist for Doctors

14.1 — Legal Literacy Is Financial Protection

Doctors operate under multiple regulators, rising litigation, high public scrutiny, and emotional patient environments. One legal lapse can destroy years of goodwill, reputation, and financial stability simultaneously.

> **Avoiding legal damage often protects more wealth than earning additional income.** This chapter provides a practical framework across three domains: professional compliance, personal legal protection, and family and estate planning.

14.2 — Three Legal Domains

- **Domain 1 — Professional** — practice, clinic operations, and medical conduct
- **Domain 2 — Personal** — assets, accounts, taxation, and documentation
- **Domain 3 — Family and Estate** — nominations, wills, succession, and dependents

Each domain must be managed independently — but reviewed together, annually.

14.3 — Domain 1: Professional Compliance

- **Registration and licensing** — valid State Medical Council registration, Clinical Establishment registration, and specialty-specific statutory licences (BMW, radiation, PCPNDT where applicable)

- **Mandatory clinic displays** — registration number, fee schedule, patient rights, and safety notices. Reduces disputes and signals transparency.
- **Medical records** — case sheets, consent forms, OT records, discharge summaries, and prescriptions retained for at least 3 years. Longer for paediatric or medico-legal cases. Your primary legal defence.
- **Consent protocols** — procedure-specific, bilingual where needed, with risks and alternatives documented. Consent is not paperwork — it is legal armour.
- **MLC handling** — document immediately, notify authorities, preserve samples, maintain chain of custody. Improper handling multiplies liability.
- **Infrastructure compliance** — fire and electrical safety approvals, biomedical waste contracts, drug storage registers. Non-compliance risks sealing of premises.
- **Professional indemnity** — legally essential and mandatory for most hospital empanelments. Covered in detail in Chapter 13.

14.4 — Domain 2: Personal Legal Protection

- **PAN, Aadhaar, and KYC alignment** — uniform name, address, and identity details across all financial instruments. Mismatch freezes accounts.
- **Nomination updates** — review annually for bank accounts, mutual funds, demat accounts, insurance, EPF, PPF, and NPS. Missing nominations create severe hardship for families.
- **Account separation** — clinic income into clinic account, household expenses from personal account. Simplifies audits and prevents disputes.
- **Tax compliance** — timely ITR filing, accurate income reporting, depreciation planning under 44ADA, advance tax adherence. Tax ignorance is expensive.

- **GST** — medical services are largely exempt. Diagnostics, pharmacy sales, and packaged services may attract GST. Confirm applicability with your CA.
- **Property due diligence** — title deed, encumbrance certificate, layout sanctions, and RERA registration verified before any purchase. Property legal errors cripple financial plans.
- **Loan documentation** — co-borrower clarity, collateral, insurance, and spousal consent documented for every loan.

14.5 — Domain 3: Family and Estate

- **Will** — ensures clarity, speed, and minimal disputes at succession. Cost is small. Impact is permanent.
- **Power of attorney** — specific POA for travel, emergencies, or overseas assignments. Never blanket.
- **Guardianship for minors** — essential for doctors in high-risk specialties. Assumptions are not legal instructions.
- **Digital asset planning** — banking access, investment logins, and EMR platform credentials documented securely for family. Prevents operational paralysis when it matters most.

14.6 — Common Legal Mistakes

- No professional indemnity cover
- No will or outdated nominations
- Property purchased without independent title verification
- Clinic and personal accounts mixed with weak tax discipline
- Poor medical record maintenance — the most common and most costly mistake
- Informal investment participation without documentation or exit clarity

Each mistake compounds risk. Each is preventable.

14.7 — Three Doctors, Three Legal Lessons

Dr. Shalini — Gynaecologist, Warangal

Bought a pre-launch apartment without independent legal verification. A land dispute emerged and locked capital for years. Goals were delayed and stress escalated. Property without legal diligence becomes a liability, not an asset.

Dr. Prakash — Spine Surgeon, Guwahati

Passed away without a will or updated nominations. His family struggled with access to accounts and investments for nearly two years. A single afternoon of estate planning would have prevented it. Wills and nominations are acts of responsibility, not pessimism.

Dr. Latha — Dermatologist, Mumbai

Faced a negligence complaint after a disputed outcome. Professional indemnity insurance covered legal fees and settlement costs entirely. Practice continuity was preserved. Indemnity does not prevent cases — it prevents ruin.

Three different doctors. Three different legal gaps. One preventable outcome each.

14.8 — The Annual Legal Review

Nine actions — review every year:

1. Renew registrations and professional indemnity
2. Review nominations on all financial instruments
3. Review and update will if circumstances have changed
4. File ITR accurately and on time
5. Audit medical records and consent formats
6. Verify property documents for any new acquisition

7. Maintain digital backups of all critical records
8. Review equipment AMC contracts
9. Review staff contracts and compliance obligations

A legally secure doctor makes clearer, bolder, and cleaner financial decisions.

Chapter 15

Taxation for Doctors

15.1 — Tax Planning Is a Silent Wealth Multiplier

Most Indian doctors lose 20–40% of potential wealth due to inefficient tax structuring — not illegality, but poorly organised income, clinic operations, investments, and expenses.

> **Tax planning is not about saving tax.** It is about structuring income so wealth compounds faster with lower friction. Post-tax XIRR is the only XIRR that matters.

15.2 — Three Income Types Doctors Must Understand

- **Professional income** — consultations, procedures, visiting fees, referrals, teleconsultations — taxed as professional income
- **Business income** — clinics, diagnostic centres, day-care facilities, pharmacies — taxed as business income with wider deductions
- **Investment income** — equity, mutual funds, REITs, PMS, AIF, SIF, debt funds — taxation depends on asset class and holding period

Doctors must understand all three to optimise tax structure effectively.

15.3 — Section 44ADA: The Doctor's Most Powerful Tax Tool

Applicable to individual doctors with professional income below ₹50 lakh. Declare 50% of gross receipts as profit. Tax applies only on that 50% — no books maintained, no audit required.

Example: Income ₹40 lakh → Taxable income ₹20 lakh → Tax at 30% bracket: **₹6 lakh vs ₹12 lakh without 44ADA**

Not suitable for: LLPs or private limited entities, or clinics with significant business income — these require regular taxation with full books.

15.4 — Business Taxation: Key Deductions and Depreciation

If your clinic earns OPD, procedure, diagnostic, or pharmacy income, business taxation allows deductions that 44ADA does not:

- **Operating deductions** — clinic rent, staff salaries, utilities, consumables, software, marketing, CME, and GST where applicable
- **Equipment depreciation** — ultrasound, dental chairs, OT equipment, lasers, X-ray machines, computers. Depreciation shields taxable income for nearly a decade, not just the purchase year.

Depreciation is a core tax shield for any doctor running a capital-intensive clinic. Missing it is voluntary tax overpayment.

15.5 — TDS: Avoiding Double Taxation

Hospitals deduct TDS at 10% on professional fees and procedures, 2% on contracts, and 1% on rent. Doctors must collect Form 16A, reconcile all deductions via Form 26AS, and claim full credit in the ITR.

> **Missed TDS credit = tax paid twice.** This is voluntary loss, not an obligation.

15.6 — Advance Tax: The Most Ignored Obligation

Advance tax applies when tax liability exceeds ₹10,000. Due dates: 15 June, 15 September, 15 December, 15 March. Delays attract interest, notices, and avoidable stress. A simple tax calendar eliminates this friction entirely.

15.7 — How Investments Are Taxed

The holding period is not just a timeline — it is a tax decision.

- **Equity mutual funds and shares** — STCG (<1 year) at 20% · LTCG (>1 year) at 12.5% above ₹1 lakh — highly tax-efficient
- **Debt mutual funds** — taxed at slab rate — useful for liquidity parking
- **Hybrid funds** — equity taxation if ≥35% equity; debt taxation if <35% equity
- **REITs and InvITs** — interest at slab rate · dividends and capital gains tax-efficient for income-seeking investors
- **PMS and AIF** — Category I & II pass-through to investor · Category III taxed at fund level
- **SIFs** — taxed based on underlying strategy — similar to mutual fund treatment
- **International funds** — taxed as debt (slab rate) — valuable for diversification despite tax drag

Tax drag is silent but powerful. Every percentage lost to tax reduces the base on which compounding works. Structure for post-tax return, not headline return.

15.8 — NRI Taxation Essentials

- **Income rules** — foreign income taxed abroad; Indian income and capital gains taxed in India
- **Account structure** — NRE accounts for foreign earnings (tax-free in India) · NRO for Indian income · FATCA and TDS compliance mandatory
- **DTAA** — Double Taxation Avoidance Agreements prevent double taxation on the same income across jurisdictions
- **RNOR window** — returning NRI doctors get 2–3 years of RNOR status — a rare tax-efficiency window for restructuring assets. Missing it is costly.

15.9 — What Works and What Does Not

Strategies that consistently improve post-tax wealth:

- Use 44ADA if eligible — the single highest-impact tax move for most individual doctors
- Claim all business deductions and depreciation — do not leave legitimate shields unclaimed
- Reconcile TDS credits every quarter, not just at filing time
- Prefer equity and REITs for long-term compounding — most tax-efficient asset classes
- Use SWP over interest income in retirement — lower effective tax rate

Common mistakes that quietly erode returns:

- Mixing clinic and personal income in the same account
- Buying insurance products for Section 80C — one of the most expensive tax-saving habits
- Overusing FDs — fully taxable, low return, no compounding advantage
- Blind reliance on a CA without understanding the basics
- Missing depreciation and advance tax — both entirely preventable

15.10 — Four Doctors, Four Tax Lessons

Dr. Neha — Dermatologist, Thane

Earned ₹38 lakh but used regular taxation instead of 44ADA. After restructuring, taxable income dropped sharply without any change in workload. Higher surplus, same income. Many doctors overpay tax simply through lack of awareness.

Dr. Ananya — Radiologist, Rajkot

Bought imaging equipment but missed depreciation claims for three years. Paid higher tax on legitimate deductions that were simply never filed. Depreciation is a core tax shield — not claiming it is voluntary loss.

Both lost money to tax structures that required only a CA conversation to fix.

Dr. Shyam — Anaesthetist, Chennai

Multiple hospitals deducted TDS but credits were never reconciled. Overpaid approximately ₹1.2 lakh in tax. Ignoring TDS reconciliation is not an oversight — it is voluntary loss, compounded annually.

Dr. Ranjith — UK-Based NRI, Returning to India

Used RNOR status strategically after returning to India. Restructured foreign assets during the 2–3 year window of high tax efficiency before full resident taxation applied. RNOR is a rare window — missing it is costly and irreversible.

Both faced tax situations that rewarded prior knowledge. Both outcomes were entirely within their control.

15.11 — Before You Move On

A quick tax audit:

1. Is 44ADA being used if professional income is below ₹50 lakh?
2. Are all business deductions and depreciation claims filed?
3. Are TDS credits reconciled quarterly via Form 26AS?
4. Is advance tax paid on schedule to avoid interest?
5. Are long-term equity investments held beyond 1 year to access LTCG rates?
6. Are insurance products being purchased for tax saving rather than protection?

Tax saved is return earned — without taking extra risk.

Chapter 16

Structuring Finances as a Doctor-Couple

16.1 — A Financial Powerhouse — or a Pressure Cooker

A doctor-couple is one of the most powerful wealth-building units in India. Two professional incomes, two sets of skills, and decades of earning ahead. Structured well, a doctor-couple accelerates wealth faster than almost any other household configuration.

Mismanaged, the same setup creates leakage, conflict, and compounding stress. Two unpredictable schedules, merged tax behaviour, two sets of parents, and different spending instincts can quickly overwhelm a household with no financial structure.

> **The solution is not compromise. It is alignment — separate incomes, one financial direction.**

16.2 — Four Couple Types

- **Type 1 — High earner + moderate earner** — surgeon + consultant. Challenge: contribution imbalance and lifestyle mismatch.
- **Type 2 — Both high earners** — two surgeons or super-specialists. Challenge: lifestyle inflation, tax inefficiency, time scarcity.

- **Type 3 — Doctor + non-medical spouse** — doctor + IT professional, teacher, or homemaker. Challenge: income asymmetry and estate planning clarity.
- **Type 4 — Doctor-parents with dependent elders** — on both sides, reducing saving flexibility significantly.

Identifying your type improves financial structuring immediately.

16.3 — The 5-Account Model

- **Account 1 — Household Expense (Joint)** — rent or EMI, groceries, school fees, utilities, household staff. Contribution follows income ratio — e.g. 60:40.
- **Account 2 — Individual Lifestyle (Separate)** — personal spending, gadgets, subscriptions, gifts. Eliminates judgement and friction.
- **Account 3 — Joint Investment** — SIPs, STPs, REITs, hybrid funds, PMS/AIF, retirement corpus. Builds shared long-term wealth.
- **Account 4 — Individual Professional** — clinic income, professional expenses, CME, equipment. Keeps taxation clean and auditable.
- **Account 5 — Emergency and Safety Fund (Joint)** — 9–12 months of combined household and clinic expenses. Doctor-couples need a larger buffer given dual income volatility.

16.4 — Income Sharing Models

- **Proportional contribution** — each spouse contributes based on income ratio — fair and flexible as earnings change
- **Equal contribution** — works cleanly when incomes are similar
- **Single-income household** — one spouse pauses or earns less — requires strong estate planning and larger emergency fund
- **One earns, one invests** — useful when clinical income is volatile — the investing spouse manages the corpus full-time

There is no single right model. Choose what reduces friction and sustains discipline.

16.5 — Risks Specific to Doctor-Couples

- **Double lifestyle inflation** — two incomes accelerate expense creep faster than either spouse notices
- **Multiple EMIs** — home, clinic, hospital, and car loans across two careers can suffocate cash flow
- **Fragmented investments** — duplicate SIPs, overlapping funds, and uncoordinated allocation reduce efficiency
- **Underestimated child costs** — premium schooling and coaching escalate faster than income in most Indian cities

16.6 — How to Invest Together

1. **Cap household expenses** — at 35–45% of combined income before any other allocation
2. **Automate joint SIPs** — from the investment account on income date — before discretionary spending
3. **Divide roles** — one spouse handles large-cap and hybrid, the other handles flexi-cap and REITs. PMS/AIF jointly if suitable.
4. **Avoid duplication** — no overlapping ULIPs, redundant insurance, or repeated real estate purchases across two names
5. **Clarify ownership** — individual, joint, or child-specific — decide before purchasing, not after

16.7 — Tax and Insurance for Couples

Three tax actions specific to doctor-couples:

- Use 44ADA separately if both spouses qualify — doubles the benefit
- Split debt investments to the lower tax-slab spouse — reduces interest income tax drag
- Align equipment depreciation with the spouse who owns and operates the asset

Insurance: each spouse needs separate term, health, personal accident, and professional indemnity. Joint policies complicate claims and exits. Clinic insurance is linked to the operating spouse. Chapter 13 covers coverage benchmarks.

16.8 — Children, Family, and Estate

Plan early for school fees, coaching, higher education, and overseas studies using equity SIPs, hybrid funds, and ETFs. Avoid ULIPs and child plans. *Chapter 10 covers the SIP-based framework for education goals.*

Present a united financial front to extended family — route all financial requests through the joint plan. No major purchase without both spouses' agreement. *Chapter 9 covers this in full.*

Both spouses must write separate wills, update nominations annually, appoint guardians for children, and maintain limited (not blanket) POA for emergencies. *Chapter 14 covers the estate planning checklist.*

16.9 — Four Couples, Four Structural Lessons

Dr. Raghav & Dr. Sneha — Orthopaedic Surgeon + Gynaecologist, Nellore

High combined income but chaotic finances — overlapping SIPs, duplicate insurance, and no allocation logic. They created a joint household account and a joint investment account with role-based allocation. A ₹1.2 crore corpus in five years, with lower stress. Two incomes create wealth only when coordination creates structure.

Dr. Mahesh & Aditi — ENT Surgeon + Homemaker, Pune

Irregular surgical income against fixed household expenses created constant anxiety. They adopted proportional budgeting and automated SIPs from a dedicated investment account. Stability returned without lifestyle compromise. Single-income households need structure more than optimism.

Dr. Suresh & Dr. Divya — Cardiologist + Paediatrician, Jhansi

Lifestyle inflation stalled savings at 14% despite rising income. They imposed a household expense cap and automated annual SIP step-ups. Savings rose to 34% within two years without reducing comfort. Lifestyle creep accelerates fastest when two incomes grow together without a cap.

Dr. Aman & Dr. Meera — Both Radiologists, Nagpur

Independent investing caused duplication and imbalance — overlapping funds, competing real estate decisions, and no unified view of net worth. They consolidated into a joint allocation framework with one advisor and annual rebalancing. Better returns, clearer goals, and full visibility. Consolidation improves outcomes by removing noise.

Alignment converts two incomes into one powerful wealth engine.

16.10 — Before You Move On

Four questions for doctor-couples:

1. Are joint and individual accounts separated cleanly with defined purposes?
2. Are household expenses capped at 35–45% of combined income?
3. Are SIPs automated from a dedicated joint investment account?
4. Do both spouses have separate term, health, and professional indemnity policies?

A doctor-couple without financial structure is two high incomes running in opposite directions. With structure, it is one of the fastest wealth-building configurations in existence.

Chapter 17

Multiple Income Streams for Doctors

17.1 — The Old Belief Is No Longer True

"A doctor's income is secure." That belief is outdated. Rising competition, hospital margin pressure, burnout, seasonal OPD volatility, delayed payments, and medico-legal exposure have fundamentally changed the income stability doctors once enjoyed.

> **Financially strong doctors share one trait: they do not depend on medical income alone.** This chapter shows how to build parallel income streams without compromising clinical practice.

17.2 — The Doctor Income Triangle

- **Pillar 1 — Active medical income** — your core profession — OPD, procedures, surgeries, consultations
- **Pillar 2 — Semi-active income** — moderate time investment with scalable returns — teaching, telemedicine, research
- **Pillar 3 — Passive / portfolio income** — income independent of your time — equity, REITs, hybrid funds, PMS/AIF

This layered structure creates stability, liquidity, and freedom simultaneously.

17.3 — Pillar 1: Optimise Active Income First

Before diversifying, maximise the core:

1. **Multi-location consulting** — avoid single-hospital dependence. Two or three locations adds predictability.
2. **Develop a niche** — paediatric orthopaedics, fertility and laparoscopy, aesthetic dermatology, advanced endodontics. Niche expertise increases pricing power.
3. **Add high-value procedures** — procedures scale better than OPD volume.
4. **Teleconsultations** — highly effective for diabetology, psychiatry, and dermatology. Low overhead, recurring income.
5. **Ethical digital branding** — consistency builds referrals and reputation. Virality is not the goal.

17.4 — Pillar 2: Semi-Active Income Streams

- **Teaching and workshops** — students, junior doctors, and online audiences via WhiteCoats, DocMode, Medflix, or CME collaborations. Steady and scalable.
- **Daycare procedures and micro-clinics** — laser rooms, mini OTs, ultrasound units for dermatology, ENT, ophthalmology, and dentistry. High-margin and replicable.
- **Telemedicine tie-ups** — partnerships with Tier-2 nursing homes and diagnostic centres. Adds predictable secondary income with minimal time.
- **Medical content and curriculum** — work with pharma, med-tech, health-tech, and academic publishers. A fast-growing, well-paying segment.
- **Clinical research** — investigator fees, site fees, and trial incentives. Common among physicians, endocrinologists, oncologists, and neurologists.

17.5 — Pillar 3: Passive and Portfolio Income

This is where wealth compounds without your time. Passive income must be regulated, liquid, and transparent.

- **Equity mutual funds** — core passive engine — inflation-beating returns, tax efficiency, long-term compounding
- **Hybrid funds** — lower volatility with smoother returns for mid-term goals
- **REITs and InvITs** — real estate without tenants or maintenance — quarterly income, high transparency, T+2 liquidity
- **Gold and Silver ETFs** — no storage, full liquidity, tax efficiency — best precious metal exposure
- **PMS and AIF** — suitable for doctors saving ₹25 lakh+ annually. PMS for equity alpha; AIF Cat II for private credit; Cat III for non-linear strategies.
- **SIFs** — structured strategies with downside control under SEBI regulation — bridges MF and PMS
- **International investing** — via Indian AMCs, GIFT City feeders, or global ETFs — currency diversification and INR hedge

17.6 — Angel and PE Exposure: Advanced Only

Startup equity, unlisted shares, and pharma distribution deals carry high return potential and very high risk. The safer route: AIF Cat I or II participation via curated, professionally managed platforms. **Access without expertise is danger.** Direct angel investing without deep diligence rarely ends well.

17.7 — Traps That Destroy Compounding

- Real estate syndicates and builder pre-launch schemes
- Unlisted startup equity without due diligence
- Crypto narratives and guaranteed return promises

- Chit funds, MLMs, and social-media driven investing
- Friend-based deals without documentation or exit clarity

Each trap destroys compounding silently — not through a single catastrophic loss but through years of locked, underperforming capital.

17.8 — The 20–30–50 Formula and Burnout Prevention

- **50% — Active medical income** — OPD, clinic, procedures — primary engine
- **30% — Passive portfolio income** — MFs, REITs, hybrids, PMS/AIF — compounding quietly
- **20% — Semi-active income** — teaching, telemedicine, research — flexibility and resilience

Building this structure without burnout requires four disciplines:

- Protect clinical time blocks — income diversification must not compromise patient care
- Delegate and build systems before adding income streams
- Automate investments before exploring semi-active income
- Avoid shiny distractions — two well-built streams beat five mediocre ones

Freedom comes from structure, not hustle.

17.9 — Four Doctors, Four Income Architectures

Dr. Shweta — Dermatologist, Hyderabad

Depended only on OPD and cosmetic procedures — volatile and exhausting. Layered in workshops and automated equity SIPs and REITs. By 40, non-clinical income covered a meaningful share of fixed expenses. Layered income creates freedom without reducing clinical excellence.

Dr. Rashmi — Orthopaedic Surgeon, Surat

Seasonal surgery cycles made income uneven. Added Tier-2 teleconsulting and routed surplus into PMS and AIF. Portfolio returns smoothed cash flow across lean months. Semi-active income stabilises today; portfolio income secures tomorrow.

Both relied on a single active income source. Both found stability through deliberate layering.

Dr. Karthik — ENT Surgeon, Erode

Resisted clinic expansion pressure and focused on consistency. Equity SIPs and gold ETFs replaced speculative ideas. Passive income reduced OPD dependence and burnout over five years. Consistency builds independence faster than complexity.

Dr. Arvind — Endocrinologist, Bengaluru

Peer pressure pushed him into direct unlisted startup investing. Two failures later, he shifted to Cat II AIFs with professional diligence. Risk reduced, liquidity improved, stress dropped sharply. Access without expertise is danger. Structure beats optimism.

Both sought returns beyond active income. One through structure. One through speculation. The outcomes were predictable.

17.10 — Before You Move On

Three questions for your income architecture:

1. Is active medical income optimised — niche developed, multi-location consulted, and fees priced correctly?
2. Is at least one semi-active income stream running or in development?
3. Is passive portfolio income automated and growing independently of clinical hours?

Doctors don't win by chasing extra income. They win by building income architecture — active for today, semi-active for stability, passive for freedom.

Chapter 18

Equity Mutual Funds

A Complete Guide for Doctors

18.1 — The Core Wealth Engine

If the Indian economy is the patient, equity is the heartbeat.

Most Indian doctors earn well yet never achieve financial independence. Capital gets concentrated in illiquid property, low-return deposits, and inefficient insurance structures. Meanwhile, equity mutual funds remain the most regulated, liquid, tax-efficient way to convert India's economic growth into personal wealth — without demanding daily attention from a time-constrained professional.

18.2 — What Is an Equity Mutual Fund?

Think of an equity mutual fund as a multi-speciality medical team:

- **Fund manager** — the lead consultant — makes final investment decisions
- **Analysts** — residents who research and track individual companies
- **Companies in the portfolio** — the patients — each monitored for financial health
- **Portfolio construction** — the case mix — balanced for risk and return across market conditions
- **Periodic rebalancing** — follow-up reviews that adjust the portfolio as conditions change

An equity mutual fund is a professionally managed basket of companies built for long-term wealth growth — with results but without operational burden. Instead of picking stocks yourself, a qualified team manages selection, monitoring, and exits.

18.3 — Why Equity Funds Suit Doctors

- **Time-efficient** — no daily tracking required — the fund manager handles it
- **Low entry barrier** — SIPs start at ₹500 — habit precedes corpus
- **Diversification** — single-stock failure does not damage the whole portfolio
- **High liquidity** — redemption in T+1 or T+2 days — no negotiation, no broker
- **Tax-efficient** — tax arises only on sale, unlike FDs where interest is taxed annually
- **Powerful compounding** — 12–18% long-term CAGR historically
- **Transparent and regulated** — SEBI oversight, daily NAV, process-driven decisions

18.4 — Seven Fund Categories Doctors Should Know

- **Large-cap funds** — top 100 Indian companies · low–moderate risk · ~12–15% long term · best for beginners and conservative doctors
- **Flexi-cap funds** — dynamic allocation across market caps · moderate risk · ~15–18% · ideal core holding – the general physician of portfolios
- **Multi-cap funds** — mandatory diversification across large, mid, and small caps · moderate–high risk · balanced exposure across cycles
- **Mid-cap funds** — future large-cap leaders · high risk · ~14–20% · best for goals beyond 7 years

- **Small-cap funds** — early-stage companies · very high risk · ~15–25% · limit allocation to 20–25%
- **Sectoral and thematic funds** — single-sector exposure with high volatility · only for advisor-led strategies with defined exit plans
- **ELSS** — 3-year lock-in with tax deduction under 80C · largely irrelevant for high-income doctors in the new tax regime

18.5 — SIP, STP, and Lumpsum: How Doctors Should Invest

- **SIP — Systematic Investment Plan** — a fixed amount invested at regular intervals. Converts income into equity ownership quietly and consistently through rupee-cost averaging. Best suited for regular income and long-term wealth creation.
- **STP — Systematic Transfer Plan** — park a lump sum in a liquid or debt fund, then transfer gradually into equity over months. Reduces entry timing risk and emotional volatility. Ideal for bonuses, property sale proceeds, or large inflows.
- **Lumpsum** — avoid one-shot investing in volatile markets. Prefer STP-based deployment with advisor guidance. The exception: markets in a sharp correction with a long investment horizon.

Most doctors are better served by SIPs than by timing the market. A consistent SIP through cycles outperforms intermittent lumpsum investing in most historical periods.

18.6 — Risk, Reward, and Taxation

- **Risk** — volatility is normal in equity — it is not the same as permanent loss. The risk that matters is being unable to stay invested through the volatility.
- **Reward** — 12–18% long-term CAGR historically. Chapter 4 shows how this compares to every other asset class after inflation and costs.
- **Liquidity** — highly liquid except ELSS. Exit load usually less than 1% within the first year.
- **Taxation** — LTCG above ₹1 lakh taxed at 12.5% after 1 year | STCG taxed at 20% within 1 year · no tax until redemption

The holding period is a tax decision. Equity held beyond one year benefits from significantly lower tax rates. This alone justifies long-term discipline.

18.7 — Life-Stage Suitability and Model Allocation

- **Residents and junior doctors (<32)** — flexi-cap 50% | mid-cap 30% | small-cap 20% | time horizon is the greatest advantage
- **Mid-career doctors (32–45)** — large-cap 40% | flexi-cap 40% | mid/small-cap 20% | balance growth with stability
- **Senior doctors (>45)** — large-cap 50–60% | flexi + mid-cap 30% | small-cap 10–20% | preservation begins to matter
- **Doctor-couples** — joint planning with tax-slab optimisation · avoid duplication across two portfolios
- **NRI doctors** — large-cap + flexi-cap with global exposure via GIFT City feeders

SIP portfolio (₹25k–₹2L/month): equal allocation across flexi-cap, large-cap, mid/small-cap, hybrid/multi-asset, and REITs/InvITs. **Lumpsum:** park in liquid fund → STP over 6–12 months.

18.8 — Common Mistakes and How to Choose

Five mistakes that consistently undermine equity fund returns:

- Stopping SIPs during corrections — precisely the wrong moment to pause
- Choosing funds via colleagues or WhatsApp groups — popularity is not performance
- Owning too many funds — 20 funds with ₹2,000 each is not diversification, it is clutter
- Ignoring asset allocation — product selection without allocation is noise
- Exiting too early — short-term volatility is irrelevant when purpose is clear

What to look for when choosing:

- Long-term consistency over 5–10 years across market cycles
- Clean portfolio strategy — does the fund do what it says it does?
- Fund manager stability and sensible AUM
- Category fit with risk profile and time horizon

Consistency beats brilliance — every time. A boring SIP maintained through every correction will outperform most tactical strategies over a decade.

18.9 — Four Doctors, Four Equity Lessons

Dr. Tanmay — Orthopaedic Surgeon, Mumbai

Started ₹1 lakh/month SIPs at age 35 and stayed invested through every market cycle including two sharp corrections. By 45, the corpus had reached approximately ₹3.2 crore at ~15% XIRR. Consistency — not timing, not fund selection — was the entire strategy.

Dr. Suresh — Dermatologist, Warangal

Shifted surplus from an illiquid investment property into equity funds, hybrids, and REITs. XIRR improved from approximately 6% to 15.4% with significantly lower liquidity stress. Equity beats property when friction is removed and compounding is allowed to run uninterrupted.

Both had capital available. The difference was where it was directed.

Dr. Kaveri — Anaesthetist, Dharwad

Used a simple allocation — 60% flexi-cap, 20% large-cap, 20% small-cap — via SIPs and STPs without overcomplicating the structure. Corpus reached approximately ₹1 crore in 7.5 years. Asset allocation plus time compounded quietly without requiring a single tactical decision.

Dr. Vasundhara — Physician, Jaipur

Ran a 9-month STP instead of investing a large inheritance as a lumpsum. Entry risk was reduced and emotional stability was maintained throughout a volatile period. STPs protect both capital and mindset — especially for doctors who are new to equity.

Both approached equity with discipline rather than conviction about market direction. Both outcomes rewarded the process.

18.10 — Before You Move On

Equity mutual funds function like a financial ICU monitor for a doctor's wealth — silent, continuous, dependable. They track what matters, alert when action is needed, and compound quietly while you focus on medicine.

Three questions:

1. Is a regular SIP running and automated — untouched during market corrections?
2. Is the allocation across fund categories appropriate for your age and risk profile?
3. Is the total number of funds below 5 — with no duplication across categories?

Equity mutual funds reward time and process. Allocation matters more than prediction.

Chapter 19

Debt Mutual Funds

Stability & Liquidity for Doctors

19.1 — The Shock Absorbers of a Doctor's Portfolio

Equity drives long-term growth. Debt provides stability, liquidity, and predictability.

Debt mutual funds are not designed to outperform equity. They exist to protect capital, stabilise portfolios, generate steady 6–8% returns, manage short-term goals, and provide structured liquidity when clinical or personal emergencies arise.

> **Debt funds are the shock absorbers of a doctor's financial plan** — quiet, controlled, and essential. Equity builds wealth. Debt protects it.

19.2 — What Are Debt Mutual Funds?

Debt funds invest in loans given to the Government of India, PSUs, and high-quality corporates. You act like a bank — but with higher liquidity, professional management, diversified borrowers, and no lock-in. A debt fund does not lend to one borrower. It spreads risk across many, so one crack does not break the structure.

19.3 — Why Debt Funds Are Ideal for Doctors

- **Liquidity during uncertainty** — partial redemption anytime — critical during unexpected clinic or personal expenses
- **FD alternative** — greater flexibility, no annual tax on interest, and better post-tax efficiency
- **Short-term goal funding** — equipment upgrades, renovations, tax payments, travel planning
- **STP parking** — lump sums deployed systematically into equity without timing pressure
- **Portfolio stabiliser** — reduces drawdown stress when equity markets fall sharply

19.4 — Six Debt Fund Categories

- **Liquid funds (~6–7%)** — smarter alternative to idle bank balance · T+1 liquidity · ideal for emergency corpus and STP parking
- **Overnight / ultra-short / low-duration (~5.5–7%)** — capital you'll deploy within 3–12 months · minimal volatility · disciplined short-term parking
- **Short-duration funds (~6.5–8%)** — 1–3 year horizons · useful for planned equipment purchases, clinic upgrades, education payments
- **Corporate bond funds (~7–8%)** — high-rated AA+/AAA issuers · steady accrual income · for conservative doctors who value predictability
- **Banking and PSU funds (~6.5–8.5%)** — banks and government-backed entities · very low credit risk · stability-focused core debt allocation

- **Gilt funds (rate-cycle driven)** — Government of India securities only · zero credit risk · sensitive to interest rate movements · suit larger portfolios with longer horizons

19.5 — Choosing the Right Category

Debt funds differ primarily in duration and credit quality. Match fund duration to goal duration — never stretch debt beyond your time horizon.

- **Liquid / Overnight** — anytime access · emergency buffer and STP staging
- **Ultra-short / Low-duration** — 3–12 months · planned near-term expenses
- **Short-duration / Corporate bond** — 1–3 years · conservative capital allocation
- **Gilt funds** — 3+ years · larger portfolios, interest-rate aware

Taxation on debt funds follows prevailing capital gains rules. Unlike FDs, tax applies only on redemption — not annually on accrued interest.

19.6 — Two Risks to Understand

- **Credit risk** — borrower default. Mitigation: stick to Government, PSU, and high-quality portfolios. Avoid chasing yield in lower-rated paper.
- **Interest rate risk** — NAV fluctuates when interest rates change. Mitigation: align fund duration with goal timeline. Longer-duration funds are more sensitive.

Safety over yield. A slightly lower return in a high-quality fund is always preferable to credit risk or duration mismatch.

19.7 — Debt Funds vs Fixed Deposits

Feature	Debt Funds	Fixed Deposits
Liquidity	High (T+0/ T+1)	Medium (penalty on premature break)
Tax	On withdrawal only	Annually on interest — even if not withdrawn
Returns	6–8%	5–7%
Diversification	High — across many borrowers	None — single bank exposure
Flexibility	High — partial withdrawal anytime	Low — fixed tenure and amount

FDs remain suitable for elderly dependents or extremely conservative allocations. For working doctors with a 1–3 year horizon, debt funds are structurally superior on every meaningful measure.

19.8 — When to Use Debt Funds — and Four Mistakes to Avoid

Five use cases for doctors:

- **Emergency fund** — 6–12 months of expenses in liquid or overnight funds — immediate access, no timing risk
- **Lumpsum STP bridge** — use liquid fund as disciplined staging for equity entry over 6–12 months
- **Short-term goals (0–3 years)** — ultra-short, low-duration, banking and PSU, or short-duration funds
- **Core debt allocation** — typically 20–40% of portfolio depending on age and stability needs
- **Senior doctors (>50)** — higher debt allocation reduces volatility and behavioural stress during drawdowns

Four mistakes that quietly erode debt fund outcomes:

- Using FDs as emergency funds — lower liquidity and annual tax drag
- Keeping large surplus in savings accounts — no return, no structure
- Using equity funds for short-term needs — timing risk meets liquidity risk
- Ignoring duration and credit quality — both determine actual risk taken

19.9 — Debt Allocation by Age

- **Below 35** — 80–90% equity | 10–20% debt — time horizon dominates
- **35–50** — 60–75% equity | 25–40% debt — balance growth with stability
- **Above 50** — 40–60% equity | 40–60% debt — preservation begins to matter

Debt reduces drawdown stress when markets fall. A doctor who panics and exits equity at a 30% correction loses more than one whose debt allocation dampened the volatility.

19.10 — Four Doctors, Four Debt Lessons

Dr. Renu — Neurologist, Mysuru

Planned a clinic renovation with staggered payments. Parked ₹8 lakh in a low-duration debt fund instead of an FD. Withdrew tranches as needed and earned approximately 7% without penalty or stress. Debt funds suit staggered short-term expenses far better than locked deposits.

Dr. Sanjana — Paediatrician, Ludhiana

Maintained her emergency fund entirely in an overnight debt fund. When a family medical crisis arose, she accessed the money within a day without touching equity investments. Long-term compounding remained intact. Emergency money belongs in ultra-liquid debt — not equity, not FDs.

Both used debt funds for specific, time-defined purposes. Both outcomes depended on matching the fund to the goal.

Dr. Akarsh — Orthopaedic Surgeon, Raipur

Received a ₹15 lakh lump sum and avoided timing equity directly. Used a liquid fund with a 9-month STP into equity. Disciplined entry, reduced timing risk, and avoided the emotional trap of investing everything at once during uncertain markets.

Dr. Yusuf — Radiologist, Noida

Split debt allocation between corporate bond and gilt funds rather than putting everything in one category. Stable, diversified, and goal-aligned. High-corpus doctors who treat debt as a single bucket miss the precision that debt fund categories offer.

Both understood that debt funds are precision tools, not a single undifferentiated category.

19.11 — Before You Move On

Three questions:

Is the emergency fund held in a liquid or overnight fund — not a savings account or locked FD?

Is there a structured debt allocation of 20–40% appropriate for the current life stage?

Is any lumpsum being deployed via STP through a liquid fund rather than directly into equity?

Debt funds are not low-return products. They are precision instruments for specific financial purposes — and using them correctly is as important as choosing the right equity fund.

Chapter 20

Direct Equity for Doctors

How to Invest the Right Way

20.1 — Same Intelligence. Different Rules.

Doctors value control, precision, and mastery. That psychological wiring makes direct equity feel intuitive — *"Why delegate to a fund manager when I can analyse and decide myself?"*

> **Medicine rewards expertise, experience, and structure. Markets reward patience, discipline, and emotional control.** Same intelligence. Different rules. Applying medical confidence to market decisions is one of the most expensive mistakes doctors make.

20.2 — Three Ways Doctors Engage in Equity

- **Long-term investing (recommended)** — buying quality businesses with strong fundamentals and holding for 3–10+ years. This is where doctors consistently succeed.
- **Swing trading (high risk)** — time-intensive, emotionally demanding, and inconsistent. Most doctors struggle due to workload and cognitive load.

- **F&O and speculative trading (avoid)** — leveraged, addictive, and capital-destructive. F&O magnifies small mistakes into disproportionate losses and demands constant monitoring incompatible with medical practice. Avoid entirely.

Activity is not strategy. High-churn trading erodes returns through costs, taxes, and behavioural fatigue.

20.3 — Why Direct Equity Is Risky for Doctors

- **Severe time constraints** — OPD, surgeries, and emergencies leave little research time
- **Behavioural bias** — tips, colleagues, media, and authority bias distort decisions consistently
- **No exit clarity** — buying is rational; holding becomes emotional; selling is hardest
- **Poor diversification** — 3–5 stocks is not a portfolio — it is concentrated risk

20.4 — Rules and Stock Selection

Eight rules that protect capital when emotions cannot:

1. **Limit direct equity to 10–20% of net worth** — core wealth belongs in mutual funds
2. **Buy quality businesses — not stories** — fundamentals over narratives, always
3. **Avoid F&O completely** — no exceptions for busy doctors
4. **Buy systematically** — phased, valuation-aware buying reduces timing risk
5. **Ignore tips and social media chatter** — source credibility is not stock credibility
6. **Use the medical framework** — Diagnose → Investigate → Treat → Review

7. **Define exit rules before entry** — never average blindly into a falling stock
8. **Review quarterly, not daily** — good businesses do not need constant monitoring

20.5 — What to Buy and What to Avoid

Prefer: long-term compounders, blue-chip leaders, high-ROE low-debt businesses, and secular growth sectors. Quality beats excitement over time.

Avoid: penny stocks, turnaround fantasies, heavily indebted companies, governance-compromised businesses, and hype-driven narratives.

Avoiding errors creates more wealth than chasing winners.

20.6 — Direct Equity vs Equity Mutual Funds

Parameter	Equity Mutual Funds	Direct Equity
Time required	Minimal	High
Skill needed	Low–moderate	High
Diversification	Very high	Low
Behaviour control	Easier	Difficult
Suitability	All doctors	Some doctors

Mutual funds = core portfolio (80–90%). Direct equity = satellite (10–20%). Crossing 20% without discipline, time, and experience is dangerous.

20.7 — Liquidity and Taxation

T+1 settlement for liquid stocks. Taxation is identical to equity mutual funds — LTCG at 12.5% above ₹1 lakh after 1 year, STCG at 20% within 1 year. See Chapter 18 for full details.

20.8 — Four Doctors, Four Direct Equity Lessons

Dr. Arjun — Orthopaedic Surgeon, Jalgaon

Invested via colleague tips and online chatter, concentrating in weak mid and small-cap stocks. A correction triggered panic exits and losses. After shifting to quality blue-chip compounders, volatility dropped and confidence returned. Stock quality matters more than excitement.

Dr. Suhas — Dermatologist, Vizag

Picked 3–4 high-quality compounders and held patiently for 7+ years without reacting to short-term noise. Strong compounding with minimal churn. Concentration works only with quality and patience — and it demands both simultaneously.

One chased excitement. One chose quality and waited. The outcomes were separated by discipline, not intelligence.

Dr. Aditi — Anaesthetist, Kharagpur

Entered F&O trading seeking fast profits alongside a demanding clinical schedule. Losses crossed ₹8 lakh within months. She exited, rebuilt via equity SIPs and a small allocation to direct quality stocks. Leverage punishes distraction. A busy doctor and F&O trading are structurally incompatible.

Dr. Radhika — Paediatrician, Jabalpur

Invested selectively in healthcare sector leaders aligned with long-term structural growth. Compounding was steady without overtrading or portfolio churn. Sector understanding combined with time creates powerful outcomes for doctors who know their own field.

Both approached direct equity thoughtfully. One through sector conviction. One through costly trial and error.

20.9 — Before You Move On

Direct equity is like critical surgery — high reward, high risk, demanding precision. Equity mutual funds are like evidence-based medicine — systematic, diversified, reliable. Doctors can use both. Ratio, discipline, and process decide outcomes — not intelligence.

Three questions:

1. Is direct equity below 20% of total equity allocation — with mutual funds as the core?
2. Is every stock position based on fundamentals rather than tips, social media, or peer pressure?
3. Is F&O trading absent from the portfolio entirely?

Doctors succeed in direct equity when quality, limits, and discipline come before confidence.

Chapter 21

Index Funds & Passive Investing

The Doctor's Stress-Free Wealth Strategy

21.1 — Protocol-Based Investing

Doctors already make life-critical decisions under pressure every day. The last thing a doctor's financial life needs is a high-maintenance investment system demanding constant attention and tactical choices.

> **Index funds are the antidote.** Passive investing is rule-driven financial treatment — consistent, repeatable, and objective. Just as medicine relies on data and outcomes over opinion, passive investing relies on long-term market evidence, not prediction.
>
> *Index funds suit doctors who value process over excitement, and evidence over narrative.*

21.2 — What Is an Index Fund?

An index fund replicates rather than predicts. If the Nifty 50 holds Reliance, HDFC Bank, TCS, and Bharti Airtel in defined proportions — the index fund holds exactly the same. No forecasting, no stock picking, no speculation. **Managers change. Index rules don't. You always know what you own.**

21.3 — Why Index Funds Are Ideal for Doctors

- **No decision fatigue** — doctors already make life-critical decisions daily — investment decisions should not add to that load
- **Ultra-low cost** — expense ratios ~0.1–0.3% — lower cost directly improves long-term XIRR
- **No fund-manager risk** — manager changes and style drift cannot affect a rule-based index
- **Powerful long-term returns** — large-cap indices ~12—16% over 15–20 years historically
- **Ideal for large SIPs, NRIs, and doctor-couples** — simple, transparent, and easy to manage jointly

21.4 — Seven Index Fund Types

- **Nifty 50** — core portfolio anchor · low volatility · long-term stability
- **Sensex** — similar to Nifty 50 with fewer constituent stocks
- **Nifty Next 50** — future large-caps · higher growth and volatility · best for 10+ year horizon
- **Nifty Midcap 150** — pure growth exposure · disciplined long-term investors only
- **Nifty Smallcap 250** — aggressive wealth accelerator · doctors under 40 with 12–15 year horizon only
- **International index funds** — S&P 500, Nasdaq 100, developed markets · global exposure and INR depreciation hedge · via Indian AMCs or GIFT City
- **Factor / smart-beta funds** — quality, momentum, low-volatility strategies · use only with advisor guidance

21.5 — Active Funds vs Index Funds

Parameter	Active Funds	Index Funds
Investment decisions	Fund manager	Rule-based
Cost	Higher (~0.8–1.5%)	Very low (~0.1–0.3%)
Consistency	Manager-dependent	Stable — mirrors market
Goal	Beat the index	Match the index
Best use	Tactical satellite	Core portfolio

Protocol-based medicine stabilises outcomes. Passive investing stabilises long-term returns.

21.6 — Risk, Returns, and Taxation

Index funds fall with markets and recover with markets — no style drift, no manager bias. Large-cap indices have delivered approximately 14–16% over 20 years. Liquidity is T+2 with no lock-in. Taxation is identical to equity mutual funds — LTCG at 12.5% after 1 year, STCG at 20% within 1 year. See Chapter 18 for full detail.

21.7 — The 3-Index Model for Doctors

A simple, powerful passive structure that has historically outperformed most active portfolios over 10–15 years with far less effort:

- **Nifty 50 Index Fund** — stability — core anchor
- **Nifty Next 50 Index Fund** — growth — future large-caps
- **Nifty Midcap 150 Index Fund** — acceleration — long-term compounding engine

This combination requires no tactical decisions, no fund switching, and no market timing.

21.8 — Allocation by Age

- **Below 35** — 40–50% index funds | 20% flexi-cap | 20–25% mid/small | 10% thematic
- **35–50** — 40–50% index funds | 20–30% active funds | 20–30% hybrid/REIT/AIF

- **Above 50** — 50–60% index funds | 20–25% hybrid/REIT/AIF | 20–25% active

Index funds form the stabilising backbone across all life stages. As age increases, the index allocation grows — less manager dependency, lower cost, more predictable compounding.

Real estate vs index funds: after stamp duty, maintenance, loan interest, and vacancy, most real estate delivers 4–8% XIRR. Long-term index fund returns are consistently higher, liquid, and cost-efficient. Chapter 5 calculates this in full detail.

21.9 — Common Mistakes

- Holding too many index funds with overlapping indices — three is sufficient
- Exiting during corrections — index investing rewards staying, not timing
- Expecting short-term returns from a long-term instrument
- Ignoring asset allocation reviews as income and age change

Index investing rewards patience, not activity.

21.10 — Four Doctors, Four Passive Investing Lessons

Dr. Divya — Dermatologist, Salem

Built SIPs using only Nifty 50 and Nifty Next 50 and stayed invested through market volatility without switching. Corpus reached approximately ₹1.7 crore in 10 years. Consistency beats prediction — every single time.

Dr. Preethi — Ophthalmologist, Bellary

Added US index funds to her existing Indian index allocation for global diversification and INR hedge. Portfolio resilience improved without adding complexity. Global index exposure strengthens a portfolio without requiring any market knowledge.

Both used index funds as the primary wealth vehicle. Both outcomes rewarded simplicity over sophistication.

Dr. Mahesh — Nephrologist, Ujjain

Reduced frequent fund switching by moving approximately 60% of his equity allocation to index funds. Volatility reduced, peace of mind improved, and long-term returns were comparable to his previous active-only portfolio with far less effort. Less churn consistently improves outcomes.

Dr. Rathore — Endocrinologist, Ajmer

A demanding clinical schedule left no time for active portfolio management. He moved entirely to passive index investing. Compounding continued uninterrupted without a single tactical decision. Passive investing removes human error by eliminating the need for human intervention.

Both found that the less they tried to optimise, the better the outcomes became.

21.11 — Before You Move On

Three questions:

1. Does the portfolio include at least one core index fund as the primary equity holding?
2. Is the total number of index funds three or fewer — with no overlapping indices?
3. Is the index allocation increasing appropriately as age and stability needs grow?

Passive investing wins by removing decisions, not by chasing predictions.

Chapter 22

ASSET ALLOCATION MODELS FOR DOCTORS

Conservative, Balanced & Aggressive

22.1 — Allocation Matters More Than Fund Selection

80–90% of long-term portfolio outcomes are driven by asset allocation — not by fund or stock selection. Doctors often ask which fund is best. The more important question is how much to allocate across equity, debt, REITs, gold, and alternatives.

> **Asset allocation is your treatment plan. Funds are only the medications.**

22.2 — Three Inputs Before Choosing a Model

- **Age** — younger doctors can absorb volatility; senior doctors need stability
- **Income pattern** — consistent income supports higher equity; variable income demands larger buffers
- **Behavioural tolerance** — if volatility triggers panic, allocation must be conservative regardless of age

Behaviour matters more than theory. The best allocation is the one you can hold through uncertainty.

22.3 — Three Allocation Models

Model A — Conservative: for doctors aged 50+, near-retirement professionals, or those with low volatility tolerance. Target CAGR 8–12%.

Model B — Balanced: the default model for most working doctors aged 32–50, doctor-couples, and NRI doctors investing in India. Target CAGR 11–14%.

Model C — Aggressive: for doctors under 35 with a 10+ year horizon, emergency fund already in place, and high income growth phase. Target CAGR 15–18%.

Asset Class	Model A Conservative	Model B Balanced	Model C Aggressive
Equity MF (large+flexi+mid)	30%	40%	50%
Hybrid / Multi-Asset	20%	10%	10%
Debt Funds	25%	15%	10%
REITs / InvITs	10%	10%	10%
Gold / Silver ETFs	5%	5%	10%
PMS / AIF / SIF	10%	20%	10%
Expected CAGR	**8–12%**	**11–14%**	**15–18%**

Every model includes a 6–12 month emergency buffer in liquid funds and REIT/ InvIT exposure for income stability. Liquidity is protection, not optionality.

22.4 — Time-Horizon Framework

- **Anytime / emergency** — liquid and overnight funds
- **0–3 years** — debt funds + REITs/InvITs
- **3–5 years** — hybrid funds + flexi-cap equity
- **5–7+ years (long-term)** — equity MF (active + passive) + SIF

Match money to time. Mismatching timeframes — using equity for short-term goals or debt for long-term wealth creation — is one of the most common and costly allocation errors.

22.5 — Gold, PMS, AIF, and SIF: Where They Fit

Gold: a hedge, not a return engine. Ideal allocation 3–7% via gold ETFs. Avoid physical gold and jewellery.

PMS, AIF, and SIF: satellite allocations, not core holdings. PMS for concentrated equity alpha; AIF Cat II for private credit; AIF Cat III for long-short strategies; SIFs for downside-aware structured returns. Ideal allocation 10–30% based on risk capacity and minimum eligibility.

22.6 — Common Allocation Mistakes

- All equity — panic in corrections without a debt buffer
- All real estate — illiquidity when it matters most
- FD-heavy portfolio with no growth allocation
- No REIT exposure — missing steady income with high liquidity
- No advisor — emotional rebalancing decisions made under stress

Allocation errors cost more than bad fund selection.

22.7 — Three Doctors, Three Models

Dr. Prakash — Dermatologist, Nasik | Model C — Aggressive

In his early 30s, chose Model C with strict liquidity buffers and avoided impulsive property purchases. By 40, portfolio crossed approximately ₹3.7 crore. Aggressive allocation works only when behaviour and liquidity are controlled.

Dr. Madhavi — Gynaecologist, Tirupati | Model B — Balanced

Adopted a balanced allocation to manage clinic demands, family goals, and market volatility simultaneously. Steady wealth growth with low stress and predictable liquidity. Balance keeps investors consistent across cycles.

Dr. Rane — Cardiologist, Alwar | Model A — Conservative

Chose conservative allocation prioritising capital safety and peace of mind. Smooth withdrawals and long-term discipline without anxiety. The best allocation is not the highest-returning one. It is the one that can be held through uncertainty.

Three models. Three life stages. One principle: match allocation to the doctor, not to a template.

22.8 — Before You Move On

Three questions:

1. Which of the three models — Conservative, Balanced, or Aggressive — matches your current age, income pattern, and behavioural tolerance?
2. Is the equity allocation consistent with a 5–10+ year time horizon, or is short-term money parked in growth assets?
3. Is gold capped at 3–7% and PMS/AIF/SIF treated as satellite, not core?

The right allocation is not about maximum returns. It is about maximum sustainability.

Chapter 23

REITs & INVITs

Real Estate Without the Problems

23.1 — The Real Estate Belief vs the Real Estate Reality

Most doctors carry a strong emotional belief that real estate never fails and rent is stable income. The lived reality is different: delayed tenants, legal disputes, poor rental yields of 2–3%, liquidity lock-in during emergencies, high maintenance, and a real XIRR of 4–8% after costs. Physical real estate *looks* profitable on paper but silently traps capital and underperforms.

> **REITs and InvITs solve 80–90% of these problems while retaining real estate exposure.**

23.2 — What Are REITs and InvITs?

Think of direct real estate like running a nursing home — high effort, unpredictability, and constant supervision. REITs and InvITs are like professionally run hospitals — systems, governance, and processes work in the background while you focus only on outcomes.

- **REIT (Real Estate Investment Trust)** — SEBI-regulated structure that owns income-generating commercial real estate — office parks, retail — collects rent and distributes income quarterly
- **InvIT (Infrastructure Investment Trust)** — owns income-generating infrastructure — highways, power transmission, renewable energy, pipelines, telecom fibre — generating long-term predictable cash flows by design

23.3 — Why REITs and InvITs Are Ideal for Doctors

- Regular quarterly income with no tenant or rent-collection stress
- No maintenance, repairs, or society management
- Diversification across cities and asset classes
- Stock-market liquidity from ₹10,000 — exit in 2 working days
- SEBI-regulated transparency — no stamp duty, registration, or brokerage

They deliver real-estate income without real-estate friction.

23.4 — Risk, Reward, and Taxation

Risk sits between equity and debt — linked to occupancy and interest-rate cycles. Total return potential approximately 10–12% over a full cycle (income plus appreciation). Taxation: interest components taxed at slab rate · certain distributions tax-free · LTCG after 3 years at 10%. Overall, far more efficient than physical real estate.

23.5 — Why Doctors Should Reduce Physical Real Estate Exposure

Over-concentration in physical property — where 80–90% of net worth sits in 2–3 illiquid assets — creates liquidity traps, maintenance leakage, legal risk, and a real XIRR that rarely exceeds 8% after costs. Chapter 5 works through the full XIRR calculation across three purchase scenarios. The conclusion: REITs and InvITs eliminate these structural flaws.

23.6 — Recommended Allocation

- **Conservative and senior doctors** — 8–12%
- **Balanced doctors** — 10–15%
- **Aggressive doctors** — 5–10%
- **Doctor-couples** — 10–15% combined

Allocation discipline matters more than timing. REITs are income instruments — not speculative bets.

23.7 — Physical Property vs REITs: Reality Check

	Physical Property	REITs / InvITs
Ticket size	₹50L–2Cr	₹10k–50k
Rental / income yield	2–3%	6–8%
Liquidity	Very low	Very high
Maintenance	High	Nil
Legal risk	High	Minimal
Diversification	None	Multi-city
Transparency	Low	High (SEBI)
XIRR	4–8%	8–12%
Stress	**High**	**Near zero**

23.8 — Four Doctors, Four REIT Lessons

Dr. Rupa — Obstetrician, Hoogly

Held three residential flats with low yields and frequent repairs. Shifted approximately ₹25 lakh into a REIT for quarterly income. Liquidity improved and cash flows stabilised. Income works best without ownership hassles.

Dr. Saritha — Hepatologist, Bangalore

Wanted property exposure but had no bandwidth for tenants or brokers. Chose REITs and InvITs alongside equity. Property-like cash flows with zero operational effort. Bandwidth matters more than belief.

Both sought real estate income. One through physical ownership. One through financial structure. The outcomes were not comparable.

Dr. Adhish — Psychiatrist, Pune

Needed quick liquidity for clinic expansion. Sold REIT units partially within days. Expansion funded without disturbing equity investments. Listed real estate's biggest structural edge over physical property is exit speed.

Dr. Basil — Pathologist, Kannur

Wanted steady passive income with low stress. Used REIT and InvIT payouts as a portfolio stabiliser. Smoother cash flows and better balance without any active management. Income instruments reduce portfolio friction.

Both wanted income without effort. REITs delivered exactly that.

23.9 — Before You Move On

Three questions:

1. Is there any REIT or InvIT allocation in the portfolio — or is all real estate exposure sitting in physical property?
2. Is the REIT/InvIT allocation within the 5–15% range appropriate for the current life stage?
3. Is physical real estate below 25–30% of total net worth?

REITs and InvITs are the modern doctor's solution to real estate investing — real estate returns without real estate problems.

Chapter 24

Gold & Silver Investing

ETFs & Physical — The Doctor's Framework

24.1 — Scientific, Not Emotional

In India, gold is deeply emotional. For doctors it has traditionally represented stability and protection. But traditional gold — jewellery, coins, and biscuits — carries high making charges, weak resale value, storage risk, and low real returns. Physical gold often *feels* safe but performs poorly as an investment, especially during emergencies when liquidity matters most.

> **Modern formats like Gold ETFs remove most of these inefficiencies while preserving gold's protective role.** This chapter helps doctors use gold and silver scientifically, not emotionally.

24.2 — Why Allocate to Gold and Silver

Gold is not a return-generating asset. It is a portfolio stabiliser. Gold performs when global uncertainty rises, currencies weaken, and inflation resurfaces. It acts as a financial shock absorber — protecting purchasing power and steadying portfolios during equity stress. Gold rallies are sharp but infrequent, triggered when multiple risks converge.

- **Ideal gold allocation** — 3–7% — not the 20–30% commonly inherited from earlier generations

- **Silver** — more volatile, industrially driven by EVs and solar. Optional diversification only.
- **Ideal silver allocation** — 1–3% maximum

Gold won't make you rich — but it helps ensure you don't lose stability.

24.3 — How Doctors Should Hold Gold

Gold ETFs are the default investment-grade gold instrument for doctors. Exchange-traded, assured purity, no storage costs, low expense ratio, and easy to buy, sell, or use as collateral. Taxation: STCG at slab rate within 12 months; LTCG at 12.5% flat beyond 12 months.

Sovereign Gold Bonds were issued in the past with specific maturity and tax advantages. New issuances are policy-driven and not continuous. Existing holders should evaluate liquidity needs and portfolio fit before exiting.

Silver ETFs and Silver FoFs are the preferred route for silver — avoid physical silver and unregulated digital formats.

24.4 — Why Physical Gold Fails as an Investment

Making charges run 8–25%, resale deductions add 5–10%, and storage risk is ever-present. Once these leakages are accounted for, real XIRR is weak and unreliable. Keep physical gold minimal — only for social or personal reasons, not for portfolio growth.

24.5 — ETF vs Physical: The Comparison

Parameter	Gold / Silver ETF	Physical Gold / Silver
Liquidity	High	Low
Safety	High	Medium
Purity	99.5%+	Variable
Storage cost	Nil	High
Tax efficiency	**Better**	**Poor**

Doctors should prefer ETFs for both gold and silver. Financial gold beats physical gold for control, liquidity, and tax efficiency.

24.6 — Allocation by Life Stage and Model

- **Doctors under 35** — gold 3–5% | silver 1–2%
- **Doctors 35–50** — gold 4–6% | silver ~1%
- **Doctors above 50** — gold 5–7% | silver 0–1%
- **Conservative portfolios** — 5–7% combined gold and silver
- **Balanced portfolios** — 4–6%
- **Aggressive portfolios** — 3–5%

Gold and silver are shock absorbers, not return engines. Allocation discipline matters more than timing.

24.7 — Four Doctors, Four Gold Lessons

Dr. Anand — Orthopaedic Surgeon, Agra

Wanted gold exposure without locker costs or resale deductions. Built a 5% allocation via Gold ETFs and rebalanced annually. Portfolio volatility reduced with zero operational burden. Gold works best when kept small and systematic.

Dr. Nikhil — Periodontist, Belagavi

His equity-heavy portfolio felt difficult to hold during corrections. Added 4% Gold ETF and 1% Silver ETF. Stability improved, making long-term investing easier to sustain. Precious metals improve staying power, not returns.

Both added gold for portfolio function, not gold belief. Both outcomes improved with minimal allocation.

Dr. Rekha — Radiologist, Vizag

Held large scattered physical gold that was illiquid and hard to track. Retained only personal-use gold and shifted investment gold to ETFs. Portfolio became cleaner, liquid, and easier to manage. Financial gold beats physical gold for control.

Dr. Farah — Gynaecologist, Udaipur

Believed gold had no role in an investment portfolio. After equity corrections, added a disciplined 5–6% gold allocation via ETFs. Emotional stability during market stress improved significantly. Gold's real value is behavioural, not financial.

One converted physical to financial. One discovered gold's stabilising role. Both found the ETF route simpler than expected.

24.8 — Before You Move On

Three questions:

Is gold held primarily as Gold ETFs — not physical jewellery or unregulated digital gold?

Is the total gold and silver allocation between 3–7% of the portfolio?

Is any physical gold held for investment being systematically converted to ETF format?

Gold doesn't boost returns — it helps investors stay invested. For doctors managing intense professional risk and long-term wealth goals, Gold ETFs provide stability without emotional or operational baggage.

Chapter 25

INTERNATIONAL INVESTING

Should Doctors Go Global?

25.1 — Yes — But With Limits and Structure

Indian doctors often ask whether India alone is enough. The answer is yes to global exposure — but only through regulated, low-cost routes, within a defined allocation of 5–15%, and as part of overall asset allocation rather than as a separate adventure.

> **Today, meaningful wealth is rarely built without some USD exposure.** But global investing must remain disciplined — not adventurous.

25.2 — Three Reasons Doctors Should Invest Globally

- **INR depreciation is structural** — the rupee depreciates ~3–4% annually against the USD, silently eroding global purchasing power and raising the cost of foreign education, travel, and relocation. Even modest USD exposure offsets this risk.
- **India is a small part of the global market** — India represents barely 3–4% of global market capitalisation. Most innovation, leadership, and capital formation happens outside India. Global markets also reduce portfolio concentration and volatility.
- **Children's global futures** — if children may study abroad or work globally, investments must support that reality. Global goals require global assets.

25.3 — Five Regulated Routes for Doctors

- **International mutual funds via Indian AMCs** — simple, regulated, SIP-friendly, no LRS paperwork. Taxed like debt funds under current rules.
- **Global ETFs via GIFT City (preferred)** — direct USD exposure, access to S&P 500, Nasdaq 100, global healthcare and technology ETFs. Low cost, clean structure, no LRS limit.
- **GIFT City outbound funds** — Indian residents invest in USD-denominated strategies without LRS caps — a major structural advantage.
- **Regulated global brokerage platforms** — select Indian platforms allow global ETFs and fractional US shares. Only reputed, regulated brokers.
- **NRI doctors** — invest via overseas brokers, NRE/NRO routes, and GIFT City structures.

25.4 — What to Avoid

- Crypto exchanges abroad
- Unlisted foreign shares
- Unregulated overseas apps and platforms

Global exposure must remain regulated, transparent, and auditable.

25.5 — Core Global Indices Doctors Should Know

- **S&P 500** — US market leaders — core of any global allocation
- **Nasdaq 100** — technology and innovation — sectors largely absent in India
- **MSCI World** — developed economies — adds stability
- **MSCI Emerging Markets** — cyclical upside — keep limited since India is already an emerging market

For most doctors, US exposure through broad indices forms the foundation. Developed markets add stability. Emerging markets exposure beyond India should remain limited.

25.6 — Risk, Reward, and Taxation

Global markets carry moderate risk and have delivered approximately 12–15% long-term returns in mature indices. Liquidity is high through ETFs and funds. Taxation: Indian international mutual funds taxed as debt funds; direct global ETFs via GIFT City or overseas brokerage taxed as foreign equity holdings. Post-tax return matters more than headline return.

25.7 — India vs Global: The Reality

India's strengths: high GDP growth, demographic dividend, rising consumption, manufacturing expansion.

India's limitations: sector concentration, limited frontier innovation exposure, structural INR depreciation.

Global exposure does not replace India — it balances the gaps India cannot fill.

25.8 — Allocation by Life Stage and Model

- **Doctors under 35** — 10–15%
- **Mid-career (35–50)** — 7–12%
- **Senior or conservative (50+)** — 5–10%
- **Doctor-couples** — 10–15% combined
- **Conservative portfolios** — 5–7%
- **Balanced portfolios** — 8–12%
- **Aggressive portfolios** — 10–15%

Enough for diversification — without diluting India's growth.

25.9 — Four Doctors, Four Global Reasons

Dr. Karan — Cardiologist, Mumbai | INR diversification

India-only equity exposure created INR and geography concentration. Added approximately 10% S&P 500 allocation. Portfolio balance improved meaningfully. Global exposure is diversification, not return-chasing.

Dr. Sunita — Dermatologist, Bikaner | Education goal

Planned US education for her daughter and saw INR risk clearly. Built a USD-linked education bucket through GIFT City. Education planning became predictable. Global goals need global assets.

Dr. Ahmed — NRI Doctor, Riyadh | NRI structuring

Wanted India's growth with USD stability. Structured allocations across Indian equity and GIFT City global ETF exposure. Globally diversified wealth without operational complexity. Structure beats scattered exposure.

Dr. Suman — Paediatrician, Siliguri | Innovation access

Sought AI and technology exposure that India's equity markets do not offer at scale. Started long-term Nasdaq and global index SIPs. Global diversification improved while India compounding continued. Global investing is a satellite, not a replacement.

Four different reasons. Four different doctors. One common thread: global exposure used deliberately, not adventurously.

25.10 — Before You Move On

Three questions:

1. Is there any global allocation in the portfolio — even a starting 5–7%?
2. Is global exposure routed through regulated instruments — GIFT City, Indian AMC feeder funds, or regulated brokerage?
3. Is the total global allocation capped at 5–15% — not diluting India's compounding story?

Global investing is currency and geography diversification — not speculation. For Indian doctors, measured global exposure is no longer optional. It is a strategic necessity.

Chapter 26

ALTERNATIVE ASSETS FOR DOCTORS

PMS, SIFs, AIFs & Market-Linked Debentures

26.1 — Satellite, Not Core

Doctors eventually reach a stage where mutual funds alone no longer solve every portfolio need — typically when income is high but time is scarce, portfolio size becomes meaningful, and liquidity planning grows more complex. Alternative investments enter at this stage.

> **Alternatives are tools, not trophies.** They exist to solve specific portfolio problems — not for sophistication or exclusivity. They are satellite allocations, never the core. Indicative sizing: 5–15% of investable assets depending on life stage and temperament.

26.2 — What Alternatives Are and Are Not

Alternative assets are non-traditional, regulated investment structures outside plain mutual funds and direct equity. They accept lower liquidity with higher complexity, explicitly price risk, and deliver differentiated return behaviour.

They are not shortcuts to wealth, replacements for long-term equity compounding, or suitable for emergency or short-term needs.

26.3 — The Doctor's Investment Filter

Before investing in any alternative, answer three questions honestly:

1. **What problem am I solving?** — volatility reduction, diversification, income stability, or downside protection
2. **What am I giving up?** — liquidity, simplicity, flexibility — these costs are real
3. **What if this underperforms or locks money longer than expected?** — if the answer is uncomfortable, the product is unsuitable regardless of projected returns

26.4 — Portfolio Management Services (PMS)

What it is: a regulated structure where a professional manager runs a customised, concentrated portfolio directly in your name. Minimum: ₹50 lakh+.

Strategies: large/mid/small-cap equity, factor-based approaches (value, momentum, quality), or multi-asset. Some PMS providers construct portfolios using curated mutual funds rather than individual stocks — useful for busy doctors who prefer professional allocation oversight without tracking multiple schemes.

Fee structure: fixed management fee, or performance-linked above a hurdle rate with a high-water mark. Performance-linked structures align manager incentives with investor outcomes. Clarity on fee model and hurdle rate is essential before committing.

Key reminder: PMS is not diversification. It is concentrated equity exposure, professionally managed. Suitability requires high risk tolerance, long horizons, and emotional comfort with drawdowns.

26.5 — Specialised Investment Funds (SIFs)

What it is: a newer SEBI-regulated structure between mutual funds and PMS. Minimum: ₹10 lakh. Combines MF-style regulation with greater flexibility.

Strategies: long-only equity with dynamic allocation, long-short strategies, multi-asset portfolios, and derivative-based risk management. The objective is portfolio behaviour control, not stock concentration.

Doctor positioning: suits doctors who want downside control with pooled discipline, without PMS ticket sizes. Best used after the core portfolio is stable.

26.6 — Alternative Investment Funds (AIFs)

Private pooled structures with defined mandates, minimum ₹1 crore+, and limited liquidity. Most are closed-ended.

- **Category I AIFs** — startups and early-stage businesses. Long lock-ins, high failure rates, unpredictable cash flows. For doctors: avoid unless allocation is very small and horizon is extremely long.
- **Category II AIFs (most relevant)** — private credit (structured lending, collateral-backed, capital-protection focus) and private equity (unlisted established businesses, 5–7+ year horizon, back-ended outcomes). Suitable only for patient capital with experienced managers.
- **Category III AIFs** — hedge-style strategies — long-short and non-directional models for drawdown and volatility management. Use sparingly with expert oversight.

AIFs are not for income needs. They require patience, expertise, and limited allocation.

26.7 — Market-Linked Debentures (MLDs)

What they are: structured debt instruments linked to market benchmarks like Nifty 50. Payoffs depend on index behaviour within predefined ranges. Tenure typically 1–3 years. Taxed as debt, depending on listing and holding period.

"Principal protection" is often a structural illusion, not a guarantee. Protection typically comes from heavy debt allocation within the structure, not from any safety mechanism. Long-term compounding potential is diluted in the process.

Principal protection ≠ return protection. Capital protected ≠ inflation protected.

Doctor positioning: MLDs are structured return tools, not plain debt. Suitable only when the payoff mechanics are fully understood and allocation remains tactical.

26.8 — Allocation by Life Stage

- **Below 40** — 5–8%
- **40–55** — 8–12%
- **Above 55** — 5–8%
- **Doctor-couples** — 10–15% combined

Beyond these ranges, flexibility reduces and stress increases.

26.9 — Before Investing: Six Questions

Due diligence checklist — if any answer is uncertain, pause:

1. Is the structure SEBI-regulated?
2. Are lock-in period and exit mechanism clearly defined?
3. Do I fully understand the return mechanics and how payoffs are calculated?
4. Is manager or issuer quality independently verified?
5. Can I comfortably afford the illiquidity for the full tenure?
6. Does this improve overall portfolio behaviour — or am I attracted by the pitch?

For doctors, clarity, control, and composure matter far more than sophistication.

Chapter 27

ELSS & Tax-Saver Products

A Brief Guide for Doctors

27.1 — Why This Chapter Is Short

Most Indian doctors earn well above basic tax-saving thresholds. Most traditional tax-saving products — PPF, SCSS, Post Office schemes — offer low returns of 6–8%, long lock-ins, and non-inflation-beating outcomes. For high-income doctors they have limited impact on long-term wealth creation.

> **Two products still matter for awareness: ELSS and NPS.** This chapter covers ELSS briefly. NPS is covered in the Retirement Planning section.

27.2 — ELSS: What Doctors Must Know

ELSS is an equity mutual fund with a mandatory 3-year lock-in under Section 80C. In practice it behaves like a flexi-cap equity fund with a lock-in — 100% equity exposure, actively managed, SIP-friendly, and offering long-term compounding.

Should doctors use ELSS? If the ₹1.5 lakh 80C limit is already exhausted via term insurance premiums, children's tuition fees, PF contributions, or home loan principal — ELSS is not needed purely for tax saving. However, ELSS still makes sense if you want additional disciplined equity exposure. Used this way, **ELSS becomes a behavioural tool, not a tax product.**

27.3 — ELSS vs Other 80C Options

Product	Returns	Lock-in	Liquidity	Suitability for Doctors
ELSS	15–18%	3 yrs	Moderate	**Suitable — growth-oriented**
PPF	~7%	15 yrs	Low	Avoid — too long, low return
SCSS	~8%	5 yrs	Medium	Retirees only
Post Office	6–7%	5+ yrs	Low	Avoid — inefficient
ULIP / Endowment	3–6%	10–20 yrs	Very low	Avoid entirely

ELSS is the only 80C product aligned with real wealth growth. At higher income levels, compounding matters far more than marginal tax relief.

27.4 — How Much Should Doctors Allocate?

- **Old tax regime** — up to ₹1.5 lakh/year only if needed to complete 80C
- **New tax regime** — ELSS not required for tax saving — can still be used for equity exposure
- **Practical sizing** — 5–15% of equity allocation if it fits overall strategy. Not mandatory.

Most doctors are better served by flexi-cap, index, and mid-cap funds when tax saving is irrelevant.

27.5 — Guidelines and Common Mistakes

If using ELSS, four rules:

- Use as part of equity allocation — not a year-end tax fix
- Hold for 7–10 years, not just 3
- Prefer SIPs over March lump sums
- Limit to one well-chosen ELSS fund

Four mistakes that undermine ELSS outcomes:

- Investing only in March and treating it as a 3-year product
- Holding multiple ELSS funds — duplication, not diversification
- Redeeming immediately after the lock-in expires
- Assuming ELSS is safer than other equity funds — it carries full equity risk

27.6 — When to Avoid ELSS Entirely

- 80C limit is already exhausted through other deductions
- You prefer passive or index investing
- Your equity portfolio is already well-structured and goal-aligned

In these cases, ELSS adds no incremental value. Skip it.

27.7 — Three Doctors, Three ELSS Decisions

Dr. Raghav — Intensivist, Nagpur

Used an ELSS SIP primarily for behavioural discipline, not tax saving, and stayed invested well beyond the lock-in. Compounding stayed strong with minimal tracking. ELSS works best as long-term equity — not an 80C tool.

Dr. Shreya — Obstetrician, Haridwar

Accumulated four ELSS funds over time, creating overlap and allocation clutter. Consolidated into one and redirected remaining SIPs to core equity funds. Too many ELSS funds create duplication, not diversification.

Dr. Imran — Paediatrician, Chandigarh

After shifting to the new tax regime, stopped ELSS and moved SIPs into flexi-cap and index funds aligned to goals. Equity exposure stayed intact with better flexibility and no lock-in constraint. Tax products must match the tax regime — habits should not drive investing.

Three different doctors. Three rational ELSS decisions. Each based on their tax situation and portfolio structure — not convention.

27.8 — Before You Move On

Two questions:

1. Is the ₹1.5 lakh 80C limit already covered by insurance premiums, tuition fees, or PF contributions — making ELSS unnecessary for tax saving?
2. If ELSS is in the portfolio, is it being held for 7–10 years and treated as equity — not redeemed the moment the 3-year lock-in expires?

ELSS is long-term equity — not a last-minute tax fix.

Chapter 28

NPS, PPF, EPF & Government Schemes

A Brief, Doctor-Focused Guide

28.1 — Brief by Design

Government schemes like PPF, SCSS, NPS, and EPF offer stability — but for high-income doctors their impact on long-term wealth is limited: low real returns, poor liquidity, long lock-ins, and capped flexibility. This chapter is short because these products are rarely core wealth engines for doctors. Understanding where they fit prevents allocation mistakes.

28.2 — Public Provident Fund (PPF)

7.1% returns, 15-year lock-in. For most doctors: avoid as a core allocation. Capital locked for 15 years cannot respond to clinic expansion, equipment needs, or overseas education. PPF is a comfort product, not a wealth builder.

When acceptable: a small 1–3% allocation for psychological safety, or for a conservative non-medical spouse.

28.3 — SCSS (Senior Citizen Savings Scheme)

8.2% taxable interest, available only post-60, 5-year lock-in. Suitable for very conservative senior doctors prioritising income stability — or parents of doctors. Rarely belongs in a mid-career doctor's portfolio.

28.4 — EPF (Employees' Provident Fund)

Applicable only to salaried doctors in corporate hospitals. 8.15% returns with restricted withdrawals. If employer contribution is available, EPF serves as a forced debt savings foundation — useful as a stability anchor alongside equity compounding. For doctors in private practice, not having EPF is often an advantage: liquidity and flexibility matter more.

28.5 — National Pension Scheme (NPS)

NPS is optional, structured, and designed for retirement discipline — not wealth acceleration. The extra ₹50,000 deduction is the headline; the discipline factor is the real value.

NPS makes sense if: you need forced retirement discipline, value the tax deduction, or prefer a preset equity-debt allocation.

NPS is not ideal if: you need liquidity, want higher equity exposure (75% cap is a constraint), already build retirement wealth via mutual funds, or plan early retirement.

For many doctors, NPS becomes rigid and low-impact relative to market-linked alternatives.

28.6 — Government Schemes vs Doctor Needs

Doctors face variable income, ongoing capital expenditure, and higher lifestyle inflation than average households. Government schemes offer psychological safety — but not financial scalability. Wealth-building portfolios require equity mutual funds, REITs/InvITs, and structured alternatives. Government schemes sit at the margin, not the centre.

28.7 — XIRR Reality Check

- **PPF real XIRR** — ~2–3%
- **EPF real XIRR** — ~3–4%
- **NPS long-term XIRR** — ~9–11%
- **Equity MF XIRR** — 12–18%
- **REITs/InvITs XIRR** — 8–12%
- **AIF Cat II IRR** — 10–14%

Government schemes rarely match doctor lifestyle inflation, opportunity cost of capital, or long-term equity compounding.

28.8 — Suitability at a Glance

Instrument	Suitability	Reason
PPF	Low	Long lock-in, low real return
SCSS	Low	Age 60+ only — retirees only
EPF	Moderate	Salaried doctors only — foundation, not strategy
NPS	Moderate	Discipline value, but rigid and illiquid
Equity MF	**High**	**Core compounding engine**
REITs / InvITs	**High**	**Income + diversification**
AIF Cat II	**High**	**Structured, predictable IRR**
SIFs	**High**	**Downside protection + growth**

28.9 — What Doctors Should Prioritise Instead

- **Equity MFs and index funds** — core compounding engine, fully liquid, tax-efficient
- **REITs and InvITs** — steady income, no lock-in, SEBI-regulated
- **AIF Cat II and SIFs** — structured risk-adjusted returns with defined exits
- **Gold ETFs** — 3–7% hedge allocation, no storage cost
- **PMS** — only after the core MF portfolio is stable

Superior liquidity, higher XIRR, stronger inflation protection — none of which government schemes can match at a doctor's income level.

28.10 — Four Doctors, Four Government Scheme Decisions

Dr. Verma — Cardiologist, Delhi | PPF

Invested ₹1.5 lakh yearly in PPF out of habit despite needing capital flexibility. Redirected gradually into equity SIPs and added REIT exposure. Portfolio CAGR improved from approximately 7% to 12%. Safety habits should not dominate a growth-stage portfolio.

Dr. Ramani — Radiologist, Mangalore | EPF

A salaried hospital radiologist, she treats EPF as her stability anchor while building equity wealth through flexi-cap and index funds. Debt stability and equity compounding coexist without over-locking capital. EPF is a foundation, not a retirement strategy.

Dr. Sathappan — Nephrologist, Kannur | NPS

Considered NPS mainly for the extra tax deduction but recognised the liquidity trade-off was significant. Prioritised long-term equity instead. Wealth remained goal-driven without rigid lock-ins. Do not lock money for marginal tax relief.

Dr. Meera — Dermatologist, Panchakula | SCSS

Her parents use SCSS for retirement income — appropriate for their age and risk profile. Her own plan focuses on equity funds, REITs, and selective AIF exposure. Two generations, two allocations, each aligned to life stage. Your portfolio must reflect your stage, not your parents'.

Government schemes are stability tools — your wealth engine still needs equity.

28.11 — Before You Move On

Two questions:

1. Is any capital locked in PPF, NPS, or government schemes beyond what is needed for stability or tax benefit — capital that would compound more effectively in equity or REITs?
2. Is the allocation to government schemes treated as a foundation (small and deliberate) or as a default — driven by habit rather than strategy?

Government schemes provide safety, not scalability. Use them selectively — for comfort, not compounding.

Chapter 29

Building a Pension Fund for Doctors

SWPs, Hybrid Funds & Pension Plans

29.1 — Why Doctors Need Their Own Pension Fund

Doctors do not inherit structured pensions. Clinical income tapers gradually while lifestyle costs remain structurally high. Retirement must be self-engineered — not assumed.

> *"Retirement: When cashflow matters more than net worth."*
>
> **The size of your pension corpus determines whether you practise by choice or by necessity.**

29.2 — What a Doctor's Pension Fund Must Deliver

- Predictable monthly income — independent of OPD volume, manageable late in life
- Inflation-adjusted growth — doctor retirement inflation runs at 8–10%, not headline CPI
- Full liquidity — unlike NPS or PPF, retirement assets must remain accessible and flexible

- Capital safety with controlled volatility — a 50% drawdown at age 62 is unacceptable
- Tax-efficient withdrawals — SWPs are structurally superior to fully taxable interest income

Retirement is not about maximising returns — it is about protecting independence.

29.3 — Three Pillars of the Pension System

- **Pillar 1 — Hybrid and Balanced Advantage Funds** — the pension engine: lower volatility, automatic rebalancing, tax-efficient, SWP-ready
- **Pillar 2 — SWP from large-cap and flexi-cap equity funds** — the monthly income generator
- **Pillar 3 — AMC pension plans (optional)** — useful only for forced discipline; hybrid + SWP is superior

Optional supplements: REIT and InvIT income, Category II AIF, and SIF exposure.

29.4 — Pillar 1: Hybrid and Balanced Advantage Funds

Hybrid funds combine equity and debt through dynamic allocation. Equity provides inflation protection; debt moderates volatility. Expected long-term return: 9–12% CAGR with materially lower drawdowns than pure equity. The ideal structure for SWP withdrawals in later life.

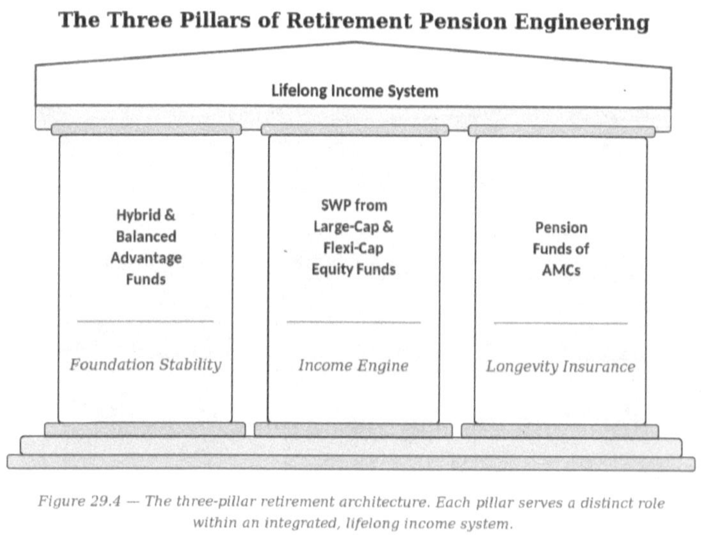

Figure 29.4 — The three pillars together transform accumulated corpus into a predictable lifelong income stream.

29.5 — Pillar 2: SWP — The Monthly Pension Generator

An SWP withdraws a fixed amount at defined intervals from a mutual fund while remaining capital stays invested and compounds. It converts accumulated wealth into controlled, tax-efficient cash flow without locking money into an irreversible annuity.

- Predictable monthly income
- Only the capital gains portion is taxed — not the full withdrawal
- Remaining capital continues compounding
- Full liquidity and flexibility
- No forced annuity — unlike NPS
- Legacy capital remains intact

"Retirement: The art of making sure your money dies after you do."

Sustainable SWP rate: 4–8% of corpus. Example: ₹3 crore corpus at 8% SWP = ₹2 lakh/month. Sustainability requires long-term portfolio returns to exceed the withdrawal rate.

Feature	SWP	Annuity
Liquidity	Full	Nil / Very low
Returns	10–14%	5–6%
Taxation	Capital gains only	Fully taxable
Flexibility	High	Rigid
Legacy capital	**Preserved**	**Limited / Nil**

29.6 — Building the Corpus: Three Methods

Method 1 — Withdrawal Rate Method

Required corpus = Annual expense ÷ sustainable withdrawal rate. At ₹24 lakh/year expenses and 6% SWP: corpus = ₹4 crore. At 5% SWP: ₹4.8 crore. Lower rate → higher safety → larger corpus required. Best for near-retirement doctors.

Method 2 — The 25× Lifestyle Multiplier

Annual expense × 25. At ₹24 lakh/year: ₹6 crore. At ₹48 lakh/year: ₹12 crore. Embeds a ~4% withdrawal assumption. Simple, conservative, and widely used. Best for mid-career doctors.

> *Your lifestyle permanently determines your corpus multiple. Every permanent ₹1 lakh increase in monthly lifestyle requires roughly ₹3 crore of additional retirement corpus.*
>
> **Retirement is mathematics wearing the mask of lifestyle.**

Method 3 — Inflation-Adjusted Projection

Project retirement expenses forward using doctor inflation of 8–10%, then capitalise at a conservative withdrawal rate. Example: ₹24 lakh/year today, 8% inflation, 15 years to retirement → future expense ₹76 lakh/year → corpus at 5% SWP = ₹15 crore. The most realistic method for doctors in their 30s and 40s.

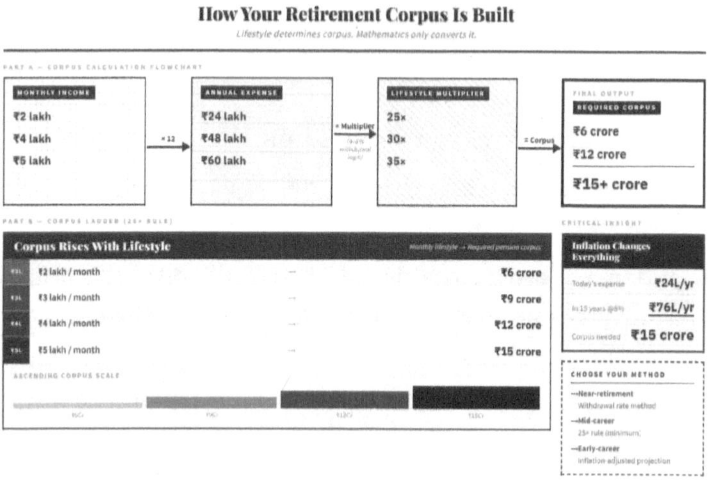

Figure 29.7 — Retirement corpus is a mathematical outcome of lifestyle, withdrawal rate, and inflation. Optimism about any one variable creates the retirement gap.

29.7 — Phase-Based Strategy

- **Phase 1 — Accumulation (Age 30–45)** — 60–80% equity | SIP + step-up SIP | gold 3–5% | PMS/AIF/SIF 5–10%
- **Phase 2 — De-risking (Age 45–55)** — shift 20–40% to hybrid/ BAFs | add private credit with 1-year liquidity buffer | maintain equity core
- **Phase 3 — Distribution (Age 55–70)** — start SWPs from hybrid + BAFs | maintain 30–50% equity cushion | add REITs and private credit | avoid annuities

29.8 — What Not to Do

- Depend on rental real estate — low yield, vacancy risk, and operational stress
- Use FDs as pension tools — tax-inefficient, low real return
- Rely only on NPS — rigid structure, compulsory annuity, 75% equity cap

- Stay fully in equity at 60 — sequence-of-returns risk is real
- Use ULIPs or traditional plans — poor returns, long lock-ins, no flexibility

29.9 — Model Pension Portfolios

- **Conservative** — 40% Hybrid | 20% Equity Savings | 20% Private Credit | 20% Gold/REITs | SWP from hybrid
- **Balanced (most suitable)** — 50% Hybrid/BAFs | 20% Flexi-cap | 10% Private Credit | 10% REITs | 10% Gold/SIF | SWP primarily from hybrid
- **Aggressive (<50)** — 60% Equity | 20% Hybrid | 10% REITs | 10% SIF/AIF | SWP only after corpus stabilises

29.10 — Four Doctors, Four Retirement Lessons

Dr. Santosh — Pulmonologist, Bangalore

Had ₹3 crore across equity, FDs, and rental property but no structured retirement cashflow plan. Shifted to hybrid funds + REITs + private credit and started a ₹1.8 lakh/month SWP. Clinic earnings turned optional. Retirement requires cashflow design, not just corpus size.

Dr. Aditya — Cardiologist, Sangli

Delayed retirement planning due to EMIs and lifestyle spending. Began step-up SIPs with a defined ₹6–7 crore target and a de-risking plan post-55. Retirement became measurable and timeline-driven. Early structure reduces late-life pressure.

Same clinical specialty tier. Both had corpus — only one had a system for converting it into income.

Dr. Sumithra — Gynaecologist, Meerut

Depended on two rental flats for income but faced vacancies and management hassles. Sold one property and moved proceeds to REITs and hybrid SWP. Cashflow stabilised and liquidity improved. Listed real estate replaces rental friction.

Dr. Indira — Radiologist, Cuttack

Wanted growth but struggled with deep equity drawdowns. Built a core equity + hybrid base with measured SIF exposure for downside control. Behaviour improved and retirement planning felt sustainable. The best retirement portfolio is one you can hold through volatility.

Same procedural specialty tier. Both redesigned retirement structure around their behavioural reality, not just their financial target.

29.11 — Before You Move On11

Three questions:

3. Which corpus calculation method applies to your current life stage — withdrawal rate, 25× rule, or inflation-adjusted projection?
4. Is there a defined de-risking plan — or is the portfolio still entirely in accumulation mode regardless of age?
5. Is SWP built into the retirement plan as the income mechanism — or is retirement income still assumed rather than engineered?

A pension fund is built through structure, discipline, and de-risking — not hope. Retirement is when you work because it excites you, not because it feeds you.

Chapter 30

Financial Goals for Doctors

Mapped to Life Stages

30.1 — Why Doctors Need a Separate Goal Framework

Salaried professionals: salary → promotion → retirement → pension.

Doctors: long education → delayed earnings → rapid income rise → volatile mid-career → lifestyle expansion → late income peak → uncertain slowdown → self-funded retirement.

Generic financial planning fails doctors. They need a life-stage blueprint — not a product checklist.

30.2 — The Doctor's Financial Lifecycle

- **Age 25–30** — specialisation, loans, low savings, minimal investing
- **Age 30–40** — rising income, lifestyle expansion, marriage, first clinic, home pressure
- **Age 40–50** — peak earnings, higher taxes, education funding, real estate temptations
- **Age 50–60** — income volatility, slowing practice, health risks, pension preparation
- **Age 60–75** — portfolio-dependent income, rising medical costs, liquidity priority

Goals must match stage — not salary.

30.3 — Seven Goal Buckets

1. **Safety** — emergency fund, insurance
2. **Short-term** — clinic setup, equipment, vehicles
3. **Medium-term** — children's education, home upgrades
4. **Long-term** — wealth creation and passive income
5. **Retirement** — pension and SWP planning
6. **Legacy** — parents' care, succession, philanthropy
7. **Aspirational** — travel, second home, phased retirement

Each bucket requires different risk, liquidity, and time horizon.

30.4 — Goal 1: Emergency and Safety

Target: **9–12 months** of combined expenses in liquid funds. Salaried doctors: 6–9 months. Private practice: 12–18 months.

Cover: term insurance, health insurance with super top-up, and professional indemnity. Doctors face medico-legal risk, unpredictable patient flows, and practice downtime.

Without safety, every other goal collapses.

30.5 — Goal 2: Clinic Setup and Professional Growth

Typical costs: small clinic ₹15–40L, mid-scale ₹40–80L, equipment setups ₹20–70L.

Build a rolling professional corpus via SIPs for upgrades and short-duration debt funds for near-term needs. Borrow only when ROI exceeds loan cost. Never liquidate long-term investments for clinic spending.

30.6 — Goal 3: Children's Education

Children's education is not an emotional goal. It is a high-inflation capital event. Education inflation runs at 10–12% — not 6%. *If retirement is slow inflation, education is fast inflation.*

Step 1 — Project the Future Cost

Future cost = Present cost × $(1 + \text{inflation})^n$. ₹1 crore today, 12 years away at 10% inflation → ₹3.1 crore. A ₹1 crore goal today becomes a ₹3+ crore obligation in a decade.

Step 2 — Reverse-Engineer the SIP

Target ₹3 crore in 12 years at 12% CAGR → required SIP approximately ₹94,000/month. Lower return assumption or delayed start raises this sharply.

Step 3 — De-Risk as the Goal Nears

- **10+ years away** — 70–80% equity, 15–20% hybrid, 3–5% gold
- **3–5 years away** — gradually reduce equity, protect accumulated capital
- **0–3 years away** — shift largely to short-duration debt — capital protection first

For overseas education: maintain 20–40% of the education corpus in USD-linked exposure to offset INR depreciation risk.

- Avoid: child ULIPs, guaranteed plans, lock-in instruments, fully equity allocation near payout

> *One foreign degree can equal 10–12 years of disciplined SIP. Education funding requires liquidity, flexibility, and structure — not insurance wrappers.*

30.7 — Goal 4: Buying a Home

Metro real estate XIRR: ~5–7% after costs with poor liquidity. Buy one home for stability. Avoid real estate as investment — use REITs and AIF Cat II instead. Funding: 5+ year horizon in 50–60% equity; shift to debt 18–24 months before purchase. Emergency fund stays untouched.

30.8 — Goal 5: Wealth Accumulation

Doctors aim for financial freedom and the option to slow down by 50–55. In peak earning years: 60–80% equity via flexi-cap + index + mid-cap funds. Add PMS/AIF/SIF selectively after surplus. REITs for yield and diversification. Expected long-term XIRR: 12–16% — wealth doubling roughly every 4–6 years with discipline.

30.9 — Goal 6: Retirement and Pension

Detailed in Chapter 29: Building a Pension Fund for Doctors.

30.10 — Goal 7: Legacy, Succession, and Philanthropy

Objectives: supporting children, caring for parents, philanthropy, structured giving.

- **Near-term bequests** — liquid and short-duration debt funds
- **Long-term legacy** — equity MFs + REITs
- **Legal** — clear wills, updated nominations, trusts where required

Legacy planning must reflect life stage — not emotion.

30.11 — Life-Stage Blueprint

Age	Key Focus	Instruments	Allocation Style
25–30	Safety & loans	Liquid + insurance	80% safety
30–40	Clinic, home, education	Equity SIPs + hybrid	60–80% equity
40–50	Wealth expansion	Equity + REITs + AIF	60–70% equity
50–60	De-risking	Hybrid + REITs + SIFs	40–50% equity
60–75	**Income & SWP**	**Hybrid + debt**	**20–40% equity**

30.12 — Four Doctors, Four Goal-Planning Lessons

Dr. Kavya — Gynaecologist, Shimoga

Had parallel goals — schooling, home upgrade, second clinic — but one generic SIP. Created goal-specific buckets and redirected property EMIs into equity and hybrid funds. Clarity improved and each goal aligned with its timeline. Bucketing converts income into outcomes.

Dr. Ananya — Orthopaedic Surgeon, Ranchi

Estimated overseas education at ₹1.2 crore in today's terms, began early equity-heavy SIPs, and planned gradual de-risking as the goal neared. Education funding became predictable. Early investing plus timely de-risking ensures certainty.

Both had income. Only one had a structure that matched goals to timelines.

Dr. Mahato — Dermatologist, Itarsi

Planned clinic expansion in 2–4 years without disturbing long-term equity. Built a hybrid + short-duration debt bucket for the specific goal. Expansion was funded smoothly without touching the core portfolio. Short-term goals need separate buckets.

Dr. Aditya & Dr. Namrata — Doctor Couple, Amaravati

Had overlapping SIPs and unclear goal ownership across two incomes. Shifted to a unified goal map with simplified equity, REIT, and selective AIF Cat II exposure. Duplication reduced and control improved. Coordination converts combined income into clarity.

Goals fail not due to lack of income — but due to lack of mapping.

30.13 — Before You Move On

Three questions:

1. Are your financial goals organised into named buckets with defined timelines, target amounts, and allocated instruments — or is everything flowing into one generic SIP?
2. Has the education corpus been projected using 10–12% inflation — not today's fees?
3. Is de-risking built into the plan as goals approach — or is the entire portfolio in accumulation mode regardless of timeline?

Life-stage goal planning converts high income into clarity, control, and long-term freedom.

Chapter 31

Model Portfolios for Doctors

SIP-Based Investing

31.1 — Why Doctors Need Model Portfolios

Most doctors invest randomly — a friend suggests a fund, a relationship manager pushes a top performer, no clarity on allocation, no clarity on expected XIRR. The result: portfolio overlap, avoidable volatility, and inconsistent outcomes.

> **Doctors don't need the best fund.** They need the right combination of funds — each with a defined role, aligned to goals, and controlling risk.

31.2 — Six Core Principles

1. **Equity is the engine** — not the entire vehicle
2. **Asset allocation matters more than fund selection** — always
3. **Liquidity is non-negotiable for doctors** — clinic needs do not wait for markets
4. **Volatility is acceptable, permanent loss is not** — disciplined rebalancing protects outcomes

5. **XIRR and real returns matter more than headline CAGR** — post-tax, post-inflation
6. **Rebalancing improves outcomes** — trim winners, top up laggards, annually

These portfolios are templates, not prescriptions.

31.3 — Four Portfolio Buckets

- **Bucket 1 — Core Equity (Stability)** — index funds, large-cap, flexi-cap — lower volatility, long-term compounding
- **Bucket 2 — Growth Equity (Alpha)** — mid-cap, limited small-cap, active strategies — higher volatility, higher potential
- **Bucket 3 — Stability and Income** — balanced advantage/ hybrid funds, REITs/InvITs — volatility smootheners
- **Bucket 4 — Tactical/Alternatives** — SIFs, Category II AIFs, limited thematic — asymmetric return profile

Each bucket has a defined role. No overlap.

31.4 — Model 1: Young Doctor / Early Career

Age 25–32 · Resident or junior consultant · Expected XIRR: 13–15%

Objective: build investing habit, maximise long-term compounding, ignore short-term volatility.

- **40% — Nifty 50 / Nifty 500 Index** — core stability
- **30% — Flexi-cap Fund** — active alpha
- **20% — Mid-cap Fund** — growth acceleration
- **10% — Balanced Advantage / Hybrid** — cushion

Overall: 85% equity | 10% hybrid | 5% gold/silver ETF

Long horizon + index discipline absorb volatility. Mid-cap accelerates growth. Hybrid adds stability without reducing compounding.

31.5 — Model 2: Early Practice Doctor

Age 30–38 · New clinic or private practice · Expected XIRR: 13–15%+

Objective: wealth creation with clinic flexibility and balanced risk.

- **30% — Nifty 50 / Sensex Index** — core stability
- **20% — Flexi-cap Fund** — active alpha
- **20% — Mid-cap Fund** — growth
- **15% — Balanced Advantage Fund** — volatility buffer
- **10% — REITs** — income and liquidity
- **5% — Gold and Silver ETF** — hedge

Overall: 70% equity | 15% hybrid | 10% REITs | 5% gold

Equity drives growth. REIT stability supports liquidity for clinic needs.

31.6 — Model 3: Mid-Career Specialist

Age 38–48 · Peak earning phase · Expected XIRR: 14–16%

Objective: aggressive compounding, diversification, children's education readiness.

- **20% — Nifty 500 Index** — passive core
- **20% — Flexi-cap Fund** — active growth
- **15% — Mid-cap Fund** — alpha
- **10% — Thematic Fund** — tactical
- **15% — Balanced Advantage Fund** — stability
- **10% — REITs and InvITs** — income
- **5% — Gold and Silver ETF** — hedge
- **5% — SIF** — downside control

Overall: 65% equity | 15% hybrid | 10% REITs | 5% gold | 5% SIF

Active funds add alpha. REITs stabilise income. Alternatives reduce drawdowns. As education goal nears within 3–5 years, shift allocation from growth to capital protection.

31.7 — Model 4: Senior Specialist / Doctor-Couple

Age 45–55 · High surplus income · Expected XIRR: 10–13%

Objective: capital preservation with growth, retirement preparation, income layering.

- **15% — Large-cap Fund** — stability
- **15% — Index Fund / SIF** — passive + downside control
- **15% — Flexi-cap / Thematic** — selective alpha
- **10% — Small/Mid-cap** — residual growth
- **10% — Balanced Advantage** — lower volatility
- **10% — Conservative Hybrid** — income buffer
- **10% — REITs and InvITs** — predictable income
- **10% — Private Credit / AIF Cat II** — structured IRR
- **5% — Gold and Silver ETF** — hedge

Overall: 55% equity | 20% hybrid | 10% REITs | 10% alternatives | 5% gold

Lower volatility, predictable income streams, smooth transition to SWP phase.

31.8 — Rebalancing Rules

- **Annual rebalancing** — restore original allocation — trim excess winners, top-up lagging assets
- **Event-based rebalancing** — sharp market rallies or crashes, clinic expansion, education timeline change, income disruption

Rebalancing quietly enhances returns and controls risk.

31.9 — Common SIP Mistakes

- Too many funds — a focused 6–8 fund portfolio beats a messy 15-fund setup
- Chasing last year's returns
- Stopping SIPs during corrections — precisely the wrong moment

- Ignoring portfolio overlap across multiple funds
- No liquidity buffer — forcing SIP breaks during emergencies

31.10 — When to Modify These Models

- Income becomes volatile
- A large lump sum arrives
- A goal approaches its 3–5 year window
- Risk tolerance changes with age or life event

These are starting frameworks, not rigid rules.

31.11 — Three Doctors, Three SIP Disciplines

Dr. Nikhil — Orthopaedic Surgeon, Bhatinda | Model 2

Followed Model 2 and continued SIPs through market corrections without interruption. Avoided adding new funds during volatility. Portfolio doubled in approximately 4.5 years through compounding. Structure plus behaviour drives outcomes.

Dr. Arun — Dermatologist, Anand | Model 3 → Model 4

Used Model 3 during peak income years, then shifted to Model 4 as responsibilities increased. The transition was life-stage driven, not market-driven. Portfolio stability improved while growth continued. Allocation should change with life stage, not market noise.

Both stayed disciplined through different market environments. Both outcomes rewarded structure over reaction.

Dr. Shibu — Anaesthetist, Thrissur | Step-Up Discipline

Began with a ₹25,000/month SIP and increased it annually as income grew. Resisted adding random funds and kept the model intact. Built approximately ₹1 crore in 9 years through step-up discipline. Step-ups outperform complexity every time.

A simple portfolio held consistently beats a perfect portfolio held temporarily.

31.12 — Before You Move On

Three questions:

1. Does every fund in the portfolio have a defined role — or is it there because someone recommended it?
2. Is the total number of funds between 6 and 8, with no category overlap?
3. Is rebalancing scheduled annually — and is the model appropriate for the current life stage?

SIP success comes from structure, consistency, and rebalancing — not clever fund picking.

Chapter 32

Model Lumpsum Portfolios for Doctors

Deploying Lumpsums with Structure and Discipline

32.1 — Why Lumpsum Investing Is a Reality for Doctors

Doctors rarely receive money in neat monthly flows. Capital often arrives in chunks: hospital joining bonuses, arrears, inheritance, property sale proceeds, accumulated savings shifted from FDs or PPF, or NRI repatriation. The two most common mistakes: investing everything into equity at market peaks, or waiting indefinitely in FDs for the right time. Both destroy compounding.

Lumpsums reward planning more than boldness.

32.2 — Five Core Principles

1. **STP beats blind timing** — structured phasing reduces regret and behavioural mistakes
2. **Asset allocation first** — focus on post-tax XIRR, not headline CAGR
3. **Liquidity is non-negotiable** — doctors need flexibility for practice, health, and family
4. **Alternatives are satellites, not the core** — 10–15% maximum
5. **As ticket size rises, sophistication must rise** — accredited investor status meaningfully improves access

32.3 — Park Before You Deploy

The STP Principle

Park the lump sum in a low-volatility debt or liquid fund first. Deploy gradually into equity via STP over 3–9 months. This avoids both impulsive peak investing and endless waiting for the "perfect" correction.

A Systematic Transfer Plan moves a fixed amount from the debt fund to equity each month. It does not eliminate market risk — it distributes entry timing across multiple price points. If markets rise during the STP window, returns may be lower than immediate deployment. Behaviour control matters more than timing.

32.4 — Portfolio A: ₹5–10 Lakh

Young doctor / early career / Expected XIRR: 10–13%

Objective: build discipline, moderate growth, high liquidity.

- **50% — Equity** — via STP over 6–9 months
- **30% — Hybrid / Multi-asset** — deployed immediately; automatic equity + debt + gold exposure
- **10% — Debt** — liquid fund for flexibility
- **10% — Gold and Silver ETF** — via multi-asset or standalone ETF

Multi-asset funds offer dynamic allocation across equity, debt, and gold without separate tracking. Simple and low-maintenance.

32.5 — Portfolio B: ₹25–50 Lakh

Early practice / mid-career / Expected XIRR: 13–16%

Objective: accelerate wealth while maintaining liquidity and avoiding real-estate traps.

- **55% — Equity** — via STP over 9–12 months
- **20% — Hybrid / Balanced Advantage** — buffer against volatility
- **10% — Multi-asset** — dynamic allocation
- **10% — REITs** — staggered entry; high liquidity, transparent pricing, superior post-tax XIRR vs physical property
- **5% — Tactical / SIF** — only after suitability assessment

REITs over property: high liquidity, no tenant or legal stress, and often superior post-tax XIRR.

32.6 — Portfolio C: ₹1–2 Crore

Senior specialist / doctor couple / Expected XIRR: 11–14%

Objective: capital preservation with growth and retirement readiness.

- **45% — Equity** — via STP
- **20% — Hybrid / Balanced Advantage** — lower volatility core
- **10% — Multi-asset** — dynamic
- **10% — REITs / InvITs** — income layer
- **10% — Category II AIF** — private/structured credit; accredited investor status improves access quality
- **5% — SIFs** — downside control

At this ticket size, accredited investor status unlocks better-quality AIFs with stronger disclosure, custom mandates, and superior private credit structures.

32.7 — Portfolio D: ₹3–5 Crore

High-income doctor / exit event / Expected XIRR: 9–12%

Objective: wealth preservation, income layering, drawdown control, succession readiness.

- **40% — Equity** — core + low-volatility strategies
- **20% — Hybrid / Conservative Hybrid** — predictable income buffer
- **10% — Multi-asset** — dynamic
- **10% — REITs / InvITs** — steady income
- **15% — Alternatives** — Cat II AIFs, private credit, SIFs
- **5% — Cash / Liquid buffer** — liquidity first; lock-ins only on true surplus capital

32.8 — Gold and Silver

Preferred route: multi-asset allocation funds offering dynamic gold and silver exposure without storage or tracking hassle. Allocation: 3–7% is sufficient. Gold's role is volatility control, not return maximisation. Avoid physical gold and ETF clutter.

32.9 — Alternatives: Hard Rules

- ≤15% of net worth in alternatives
- Lock-ins must match cashflow comfort — alternatives must never touch capital you may need
- Exit path must be clear before entry
- Category II AIFs: structured private credit, 10–14% IRR, for patient capital
- SIFs: useful tactically in uncertain markets, defined payoff structures, downside buffers

Alternatives must add control — not complexity.

32.10 — Common Lumpsum Mistakes

- Investing everything at market peaks — STP always
- Leaving money idle in FDs for years
- Buying multiple properties without XIRR clarity

- Over-allocating to illiquid AIFs beyond cashflow comfort
- Ignoring taxation and exit timelines before committing

Structure beats prediction. Liquidity beats regret.

32.11 — Special Case: Deploying Proceeds from an Unlisted Hospital Equity Sale

Dr. Vikram — Cardiologist, Hyderabad

Dr. Vikram invested **₹20 lakh** for a minority stake in a mid-size corporate hospital in 2016. Eight years later, a larger group acquired it. His stake was bought out for **₹1.5 crore**. The money hit his account on a Tuesday morning. By Thursday, three people had already called with "opportunities." This is the moment most doctors get wrong.

Step 1 — Compute the Tax First

Unlisted equity held for more than 24 months qualifies as long-term capital gain. Two tax treatment options are available — the choice determines the actual deployable corpus.

	Option 1: 12.5% flat	**Option 2: 20% + indexation**
Sale proceeds	₹1,50,00,000	₹1,50,00,000
Cost / Indexed cost	₹20,00,000	₹27,50,000 (CII 264→363)
Taxable LTCG	₹1,30,00,000	₹1,22,50,000
LTCG tax	₹16,25,000 (12.5%)	₹24,50,000 (20%)
Surcharge	₹2,44,000 (15%)	₹3,67,500 (15%)
Cess	₹75,000 (4%)	₹1,13,000 (4%)
Total tax	**₹19,43,000**	**₹29,30,000**
Net in-hand	**₹1,30,57,000** ✓	**₹1,20,70,000**

Option 1 (12.5% flat) saves ₹9.87 lakh here because the appreciation is high (7.5×) and the indexed cost remains small relative to the gain.

Option 2 (20% with indexation) is better when appreciation is moderate (under 2–3×) or the holding period is long enough for CII to substantially reduce taxable gains.

Surcharge (currently 15%) and health and education cess (currently 4%) apply on top of the base tax. Applicable rates must be confirmed with your CA at the time of the transaction.

A note on other outflows: if proceeds are deployed toward loan repayments, insurance premiums, or donations before investment, these reduce the deployable corpus. Donations may carry 80G benefit against income tax but do not directly offset LTCG tax. Confirm all deduction treatment with your CA.

Step 2 — Know Your Loan Position

Dr. Vikram has two outstanding loans at meaningfully different interest rates. This asymmetry is the foundation of the strategic choice that follows.

Loan	Outstanding	Rate	EMI	Tenure left
Home loan	₹50,00,000	7.5%	₹69,419	96 months
Personal loan	₹30,00,000	11.0%	₹77,537	48 months
Combined	**₹80,00,000**	—	**₹1,46,956**	—

Why the rate difference matters: the personal loan at **11%** leaves only a **3%** spread against 14% equity returns — a thin margin that barely justifies keeping it. The home loan at **7.5%** leaves a **6.5%** spread — a meaningful differential that makes keeping capital invested worthwhile rather than prepaying.

Two deployment questions to settle first: investing proceeds in another property is only worthwhile if it is the first home purchase. Capital gains bonds (Section 54EC) yield approximately 5–5.5% with a 5-year lock-in and a **₹50 lakh** annual cap — not a worthwhile deployment for doctors with long compounding horizons.

Step 3 — Park Before You Deploy

> **The 6-Month Parking Rule**
>
> Before deploying a single rupee, park the full net proceeds in a liquid or short-duration debt fund. Three reasons: (1) emotional decompression — the pressure to act is highest in the first weeks; (2) planning time — a proper deployment plan takes weeks to build correctly; (3) market entry discipline — equity entered via STP over 9–12 months reduces timing risk significantly.

Step 4 — Three Deployment Scenarios

Scenario A — Full Debt Freedom: repay both loans (**₹80L**). Deploy remaining **₹50.6L** via STP into equity. The freed combined EMI of **₹1,46,956**/month becomes the SIP for the next 10 years. Clean balance sheet, maximum SIP engine.

Scenario B — Smart Debt Strategy: repay only the expensive personal loan (**₹30L at 11%**). Keep the home loan running — borrowing at **7.5%** while **₹100.6L** compounds at 14% is a **6.5%** positive spread worth maintaining. The freed personal loan EMI of **₹77,537**/month becomes the SIP. Home loan EMI (**₹69,419**) continues from regular income.

Scenario C — Maximum Deployment: repay no loans. Deploy the full **₹130.6L** via STP. Both loans serviced from regular income. Largest corpus deployed, highest standalone corpus at Year 10 — but no SIP engine started. Highest interest cost: **₹23.9L** across both loans.

Parameter	Scenario A Full Debt Freedom	Scenario B Smart Debt	Scenario C Max Deployment
Loans repaid	Both (₹80L)	PL only (₹30L)	None
Investable corpus	₹50.6L	₹100.6L	₹130.6L
STP deployment	₹50.6L via hybrid then equity	₹100.6L via hybrid then equity	₹130.6L via hybrid then equity
Corpus at Year 10 (@14% CAGR)	₹1.82 Cr	₹3.61 Cr	₹4.69 Cr
Monthly SIP (freed EMI)	₹1,46,956	₹77,537	Nil
Total invested in SIP (10 yrs)	₹1.76 Cr	₹0.93 Cr	Nil
SIP corpus @12%	₹3.41 Cr	₹1.80 Cr	Nil
Total wealth @12%	**₹5.23 Cr**	**₹5.41 Cr**	**₹4.69 Cr**
SIP corpus @15%	₹4.10 Cr	₹2.16 Cr	Nil
Total wealth @15%	**₹5.91 Cr**	**₹5.77 Cr**	**₹4.69 Cr**
SIP corpus @18%	₹4.94 Cr	₹2.61 Cr	Nil
Total wealth @18%	**₹6.76 Cr**	**₹6.22 Cr**	**₹4.69 Cr**
Home loan running?	No	Yes (₹69K/mo from income)	Yes (₹69K/mo from income)
Interest cost	Nil	₹16.6L (HL only)	₹23.9L (both loans)

Note: Corpus projections use 10% p.a. in balanced hybrid fund for Months 1–12 (STP phase) and 14% CAGR thereafter. SIP projections at 12%/15%/18% are possible long-term outcomes, not guarantees. All figures pre-tax on future gains.

The crossover insight: Scenario B outperforms A at conservative SIP returns (12%) because the larger corpus more than offsets the smaller SIP. Scenario A wins decisively at 15%+ because the freed combined EMI of **₹1.47 lakh**/month is a powerful 10-year compounding engine. Scenario C, despite the largest corpus, finishes last every time — because the SIP multiplier dominates over a full decade.

The Mistake That Erases the Windfall

The most common error after a liquidity event: reinvesting directly into another hospital stake, a commercial property, or a business deal — usually within weeks, under peer or promoter pressure. This recreates the exact problem the exit was supposed to solve. The doctor trades one illiquid, concentrated position for another — without diversification, without income generation, and without a structured exit path.

The guiding principle: *A liquidity event is a one-time opportunity to diversify permanently. The goal is not to find the next high-return bet. The goal is to ensure this capital never gets trapped in an illiquid position again.*

32.12 — Three Doctors, Three Lumpsum Lessons

Dr. Jignesh — Physician, Mehsana | Portfolio B Band

After selling a commercial property for approximately **₹1.4 crore**, avoided reinvesting in another tenant-driven asset. Split the corpus across REITs (income), Category II AIF (stability), and hybrid funds (liquidity). Income began flowing while capital stayed diversified and flexible. Split lumpsums by function — income, stability, and liquidity.

Dr. Ritu & Dr. Aman — Doctor Couple, Delhi NCR | Portfolio C Band

Received approximately **₹3 crore** inheritance and faced pressure to buy land. Parked funds in liquid debt and deployed via 9–12 month STP into equity, adding balanced advantage and limited SIF exposure. Behaviour stayed disciplined and returns stabilised around **11% XIRR**. Phased deployment protects both returns and psychology.

Both cases: lumpsum received under pressure. Both outcomes rewarded the pause before deployment.

Dr. Kishore — ENT Surgeon, Hyderabad | Portfolio D Band

As an accredited investor, preferred predictable compounding over maximum returns. Built a measured allocation into select Category II private credit AIFs. The alternative bucket delivered steady IRR-like outcomes without liquidity strain. Alternatives should enhance structure — not chase excitement.

Same procedural specialty tier as Dr. Vikram (Section 32.11). Both faced lumpsum capital events. Both chose structure over speed.

32.13 — Before You Move On

Five questions before deploying any lumpsum:

1. What is the time horizon and liquidity requirement for this capital?
2. Has the corpus been parked in a liquid or debt fund first — with STP mandates ready?
3. Is the allocation split appropriately across income, growth, and stability buckets?
4. Are alternatives below 15% of net worth with clear exit mechanisms?
5. Has the post-tax XIRR expectation been confirmed — not just the headline CAGR?

Lumpsums reward structure, liquidity discipline, and real-return focus — not bravado. When allocated across regulated products with clear roles and exit pathways, lumpsum capital compounds steadily and converts into long-term freedom.

Chapter 33

Retirement Planning for Doctors

Longevity, Income Layers & Capital Protection

33.1 — Retirement Is a Phase, Not a Date

Doctors don't retire at 60. They slow down — reducing procedures, shifting to consulting or OPD work, becoming selective. Income becomes uneven, health-dependent, and tied to stamina. Lifestyle costs do not slow with it.

> **For doctors, retirement is not a date. It is a 20–30 year funding phase that must be engineered, not assumed.**

33.2 — Three Retirement Risks

- **Longevity risk** — doctors often live 25–35 years post-retirement. The corpus must last longer than most people plan for.
- **Inflation risk** — doctor lifestyle inflation runs at 8–10%, often higher than headline CPI. Planning at 6% creates retirement gaps.
- **Sequence-of-returns risk** — a major market fall early in retirement permanently damages a portfolio if withdrawals begin from pure equity. The order of returns matters, not just the average.

A sound retirement plan manages all three risks together — not individually.

33.3 — How Much Corpus Does a Doctor Need?

Rule: 25–30× annual expenses. At **₹24 lakh**/year: **~₹6 crore**. At **₹36 lakh**/year: **~₹9 crore**. This reflects longer life expectancy and higher lifestyle inflation. Government schemes (PPF, NPS) fall short — see Chapter 28. A self-created, market-linked pension system is essential.

33.4 — The Four-Layer Retirement Architecture

- **Layer 1 — Safety and liquidity (Years 0–3)** — 2–3 years of expenses in liquid funds. Prevents forced equity selling during market crashes.
- **Layer 2 — Income stability (Years 3–10)** — balanced advantage funds, conservative hybrids, REITs/InvITs. SWP and REIT distributions. Target return 7–10%.
- **Layer 3 — Growth engine (Years 10–30)** — flexi-cap and index funds. 30–50% equity even during retirement. Equity must keep compounding to prevent long-term corpus erosion.
- **Layer 4 — Predictable yield (optional)** — Category II AIFs and SIFs for suitable doctors. 5–15% allocation for structured income and downside control.

Retirement success depends more on withdrawal structure than raw corpus size.

33.5 — SWP: The Backbone of Retirement Income

SWP is the most efficient retirement income tool when portfolio returns exceed withdrawal rates. Safe withdrawal: **4–5%** conservative, **5–6%** balanced, **6–9%** early retirement (with caution). At **₹6 crore** corpus and **8% SWP**: **₹48 lakh**/year = **₹4 lakh**/month. Full SWP mechanics and corpus calculation methods are in Chapter 29.

33.6 — Multi-Asset Funds, Gold, and Accredited Investors

- **Multi-asset funds** — automatic rebalancing with built-in equity, debt, and gold. Ideal for doctors aged 50–65 who prefer lower-maintenance portfolios.

- **Gold** — 3–7% via multi-asset funds or ETFs. Hedges volatility; does not maximise returns.
- **Accredited investors** — high-net-worth doctors nearing retirement should evaluate accredited investor status. Better-structured PMS/AIF strategies, stronger disclosures, and improved downside clarity enable predictable income layers.

33.7 — Four Mistakes to Avoid

- Overexposure to illiquid assets — rental property cannot fund monthly expenses reliably
- Exiting equity completely at retirement — inflation erodes a debt-only portfolio over 25 years
- Starting SWPs without a 2–3 year safety buffer — sequence risk destroys early years
- Delaying planning until 55+ — every year of delay raises the required corpus meaningfully

33.8 — Three Doctors, Three Retirement Structures

Dr. Raghavan — Orthopaedic Surgeon, Chennai

Built approximately **₹8 crore** corpus and wanted income without being forced into OPD. Created a three-layer structure: 2 years of expenses in liquid funds, SWP from hybrid funds, and ~35% equity retained. Work became optional while equity stayed protected during downturns.

Dr. Neeraj — Gynaecologist, Bhavnagar

Owned two rental flats with inconsistent cashflows. Shifted part of property capital into REITs and hybrid funds for structured withdrawals. Cashflow became cleaner, more predictable, and required zero operational effort.

Both redesigned retirement income around structure rather than asset ownership.

Dr. Joseph — Physician, Kochi

Wanted stable income without over-relying on FDs. As an accredited investor, added a private credit Category II AIF layer while retaining ~35% equity. Income stabilised without sacrificing inflation protection. Structured yield layers enhance behaviour without killing growth.

Income stability and growth protection are not opposing goals. The right layer structure delivers both simultaneously.

33.9 — Before You Move On

Retirement readiness checklist:

1. Is there a 2–3 year expense buffer in liquid funds — independent of the investment portfolio?
2. Is equity retained at 30–50% to protect against inflation over a 20–30 year horizon?
3. Is there a clear SWP strategy — or is retirement income still assumed rather than engineered?
4. Are will and nominations updated and accessible to family?

Doctors spend their lives caring for others. Retirement planning is about finally caring for yourself — with dignity, flexibility, and the choice to stop.

Chapter 34

Wealth Protection & Succession Planning

For Doctors

34.1 — Wealth Creation Without Protection Is Incomplete

Doctors are exceptional wealth creators — but often weak wealth protectors. Years of effort can be undone by absent documentation, unclear nominations, sudden incapacity, premature death, family disputes, or medico-legal exposure. This chapter is about continuity, dignity, and control.

- **Sudden incapacity** — an accident or illness can instantly impair ability to practise or manage finances
- **Premature death** — without planning, accounts freeze, clinics stall, families struggle
- **Legal and tax complications** — poor structuring causes avoidable taxes and prolonged probate
- **Family conflict** — even close families fracture when authority and money are unclear

34.2 — Nomination Is Not Succession

Nomination ≠ Legal inheritance. A nominee receives assets temporarily. Legal heirs determine final ownership. Many doctors nominate a spouse, assume children inherit automatically, and skip writing a will — creating confusion at exactly the wrong moment.

Nomination is administrative convenience. A will is legal instruction. Both are essential.

34.3 — Writing a Will

Every doctor must have a will. It should cover bank accounts, mutual funds, demat holdings, REITs/InvITs/AIF/PMS units, properties, insurance proceeds, clinic ownership, equipment, and hospital equity. A simple will suffices for most doctors and can be updated at any time. Registration is optional but recommended.

34.4 — Power of Attorney

Financial PoA authorises someone to operate accounts, manage clinic finances, and handle compliance during incapacity. **Medical PoA / advance directive** authorises medical decision-making and reduces family conflict during crises. For clinic-owning doctors, both are essential — not optional.

34.5 — Structuring Assets Correctly

Joint holding with survivor clauses prevents account freezing. Doctor couples should balance ownership across both names. Partnership deeds must clearly define death and disability clauses, buy-out valuation methods, and successor eligibility — ambiguity almost always leads to disputes.

34.6 — Insurance as Risk Transfer

- Adequate term insurance — income replacement for dependents
- Health insurance with super top-up — medical cost protection
- Professional indemnity — medico-legal exposure
- Clinic insurance — equipment, fire, and liability

Insurance is not an investment. ULIPs and endowments for protection produce low cover and poor returns. *See Chapter 13 for full detail.*

34.7 — Clinic Succession

This is uniquely doctor-specific. Every clinic owner must decide who runs the practice during incapacity and whether family can manage or the clinic should be sold. Practical solutions: documented SOPs with a trusted administrator, buy-sell agreements with pre-defined valuation, and insurance-funded buy-outs.

Without planning, a clinic quickly becomes a distressed asset.

34.8 — Trusts, Tax, and Regulated Assets

Trusts are useful for large net worth, minor or special-needs dependents, philanthropic intent, or asset protection. Require professional design — not DIY.

Tax: inheritance itself is not taxed in India. Income generated after inheritance is taxable. Good structuring reduces friction.

Regulated assets (mutual funds, REITs, AIFs, SIFs) are easier to transfer, more transparent, and more liquid than unlisted holdings or cash-heavy assets. Regulation is itself a layer of protection.

34.9 — Three Doctors, Three Outcomes

Dr. Prakash — Physician, Hospet

A sudden stroke left him temporarily incapacitated with no Financial PoA. Bank processes slowed and paperwork mounted during a medical crisis. Access delays created avoidable strain at exactly the wrong time.

Dr. Savitri — Dermatologist, Mahad

Ran a profitable single-owner clinic with no written succession plan or SOPs. After a health emergency, receivables, vendors, and management fell into confusion. The clinic was sold under pressure at a discounted valuation.

Dr. Thomas — Orthopaedic Surgeon, Kollam

Maintained a clear will, updated nominations, and a partnership agreement with defined buy-out terms. When an unexpected emergency occurred, operations and access remained organised. The family faced grief without administrative chaos.

Succession planning is not paperwork — it is continuity.

34.10 — Before You Move On

Seven-point checklist:

1. Written will covering all asset classes
2. Updated nominations on all accounts and policies
3. Financial PoA executed and accessible
4. Medical PoA or advance directive in place
5. Adequate term, health, indemnity, and clinic insurance
6. Clinic succession plan with SOPs and partner agreements
7. Consolidated asset record reviewed annually

Doctors heal lives. Succession planning protects the lives they leave behind.

Chapter 35

Accumulation Phase Case Studies

Early Career Foundations

35.1 — The Phase That Sets Everything Else

Doctor earnings surge post-specialisation. The decade from 30 to 40 determines whether surplus compounds smoothly or gets trapped in loans, lifestyle inflation, and premature property. Mistakes here take decades to undo.

- **Allocation (age 25–40)** — 70–85% equity (index + flexi-cap + mid-cap) | 10–20% hybrid | 3–5% gold | 5–10% liquidity buffer
- **Target** — 12–16% long-term XIRR
- **Priority** — discipline over sophistication. High equity at this stage is not aggression — it is mathematics.

35.2 — Four Doctors, Four Accumulation Lessons

Dr. Ankit — Urologist, Ghaziabad

Income rose from **₹6L** to **₹18L**; carried a moderate education loan and faced pressure to buy land. Started **₹30,000**/month SIP with annual step-ups, maintained **80% equity**, prepaid loan methodically, and avoided real estate. Corpus: ~**₹45 lakh** in 7 years at **14% XIRR**. Early structure beats early property.

Dr. Sudhir — Dermatologist, Bengaluru

Private practice brought volatile income and pressure for a second apartment. Imposed a fixed expense ceiling, invested **₹75,000**/month in equity-heavy SIPs, chose REITs over property. Corpus: ~**₹80 lakh** in 5 years, zero EMI drag. Control lifestyle before it controls you.

Both resisted property pressure during the accumulation phase. Both outcomes rewarded the discipline to wait.

Dr. Sandeep & Dr. Kavya — Doctor Couple, Pune

₹45 lakh combined income, family pressure for multiple properties. Mapped goals jointly, allocated **70% equity**, **15% hybrid**, **10% REITs**, **5% gold** with a dedicated emergency fund. Corpus: ~**₹1.2 crore** in 6 years. High income works only when structured.

Dr. Farah — Government Doctor, Dewas

Conservative background, initially preferred FDs and jewellery. Started with index SIPs, gradually added hybrid funds and multi-asset for gold exposure. Corpus: **~12% CAGR** over 8 years with a decisive mindset shift. Comfort first, growth next — but growth must follow.

This phase isn't glamorous — but it quietly builds the financial backbone.

35.3 — What to Avoid

- Real estate too early — locks capital at its highest-leverage point
- Excessive EMIs — permanently reduce investable surplus
- Parking surplus in FDs — low real returns, annual tax drag
- Unlisted shares, guaranteed-return products, crypto — unregulated and unsuitable
- Lifestyle creep disguised as reward

What you avoid in this phase matters as much as what you invest in.

35.4 — Before You Move On

Accumulation phase checklist:

1. Term and health insurance in place
2. Emergency fund covering 6–9 months of expenses
3. Equity-heavy SIPs running and automated
4. Annual SIP step-up committed
5. EMIs below 30% of income
6. Discipline maintained through market falls

Time + equity + discipline in this decade create exponential advantage in every decade that follows.

Chapter 36

Growth Phase Case Studies

Compounding at Scale

36.1 — The Golden Window — and Its Traps

Ages 40–55 are the golden window. Income peaks, reputation is strong, confidence is high — and banks, brokers, and "opportunities" aggressively pursue you. **Large capital magnifies both discipline and mistakes.**

- **Allocation (age 40–55)** — 55–65% equity (index + flexi-cap + mid-cap) | 15–25% hybrid | 8–12% REITs/InvITs | 5–10% alternatives | 3–5% gold
- **Target** — 11–14% long-term XIRR with lower volatility than the accumulation phase
- **Priority** — risk-adjusted returns, capital protection, retirement glide path, reducing dependence on active income

36.2 — Four Doctors, Four Growth Phase Lessons

Dr. Rajesh — Cardiac Surgeon, Mumbai

At peak income (~**₹1.5 crore**/year), faced frequent commercial property pitches. Built equity core (flexi-cap + index), chose REITs over direct property, added Category II AIF for stable IRR, and used measured SIF allocation. As an accredited investor, accessed better-structured mandates. Portfolio crossed **₹9 crore** in 7 years at **12.5% XIRR** with no concentration risk. Peak income requires peak discipline.

Dr. Abhay — Gynaecologist, Delhi

Held three low-yield properties with poor liquidity. Sold one underperformer, shifted capital to REITs and hybrid funds, added private credit AIF, and structured portfolio for future SWPs. Retirement readiness improved within 6 years. Correcting mistakes matters more than defending them.

Both redirected growth-phase capital away from illiquid concentration and toward structured, diversified instruments.

Dr. Imran & Dr. Parveen — Doctor Couple, Hyderabad

Dual high incomes and large bonuses led to over-diversification and thematic chasing. Consolidated into 8 core funds, capped alternatives at **10%**, added multi-asset exposure, followed strict annual rebalancing. Stable **~13% XIRR** with cleaner structure. More funds do not mean better diversification.

Dr. Anand Babu — Orthopaedic Surgeon, Madurai

Conservative mindset led to excessive FDs and limited equity exposure. Shifted gradually to hybrid funds, added index equity, used multi-asset for gold. Portfolio CAGR improved from **~7%** to **~11%** over 8 years. You don't need aggression — you need consistency.

The compounding advantage of this phase comes from doing nothing wrong. Avoiding major mistakes adds more value than chasing an extra 2%.

36.3 — Traps and Accredited Investor Advantage

Growth-phase traps to avoid:

- Overloading real estate — illiquidity at scale
- Unlisted investments without exit clarity
- Oversized cheques driven by confidence, not structure
- Excessive alternatives beyond 10–15%
- Skipping annual rebalancing

Accredited investor status improves access to better-structured AIFs, institutional-grade private credit, and customised mandates. Accreditation improves access — not judgement. Structuring still matters.

36.4 — Before You Move On

Growth phase checklist:

1. Clear asset allocation with equity core above 55%
2. Alternatives capped at 10–15% of net worth
3. Liquidity buffer preserved independently of investments
4. Defined exit paths on all alternative positions
5. Annual rebalancing scheduled and executed
6. Retirement glide path initiated — de-risking plan in place

Doctors who respect capital, liquidity, and structure in this phase enter their 50s financially unshakeable.

Chapter 37

Preservation Phase Case Studies

Protecting What You've Built

37.1 — The Question Changes

Ages 55–70: the corpus is at its largest — and one wrong decision can undo decades of effort. The question shifts from "how much more can I make" to "how safely can I protect what I've built." Growth still matters — but not at the cost of sleep.

- **Allocation** — 40–50% equity (index, low-volatility) | 25–30% hybrid | 10–15% REITs/InvITs | 5–10% alternatives | 5–10% liquidity buffer
- **Target** — 9–12% XIRR with controlled drawdowns
- **Priority** — capital protection, predictable cashflow, inflation-adjusted income, simplicity, succession readiness

37.2 — Four Doctors, Four Preservation Lessons

Dr. Krishnan — Senior Physician, Coimbatore

Reducing OPD hours and volatility fears pushed him toward exiting equity entirely. Instead retained ~**45% equity**, built a 3-year expense buffer, and structured hybrid funds + REITs with SWP from balanced advantage funds. Stable monthly income with controlled drawdowns. Exiting equity completely is often riskier than staying invested with structure.

Dr. Suresh — Gynaecologist, Jaipur

Relied heavily on FDs but falling real returns eroded purchasing power. Transitioned into conservative hybrid funds, REITs for rental-like income, and multi-asset allocation. Inflation protection improved while liquidity remained intact. Safety does not mean stagnation.

Both redesigned preservation around income structure rather than product familiarity.

Dr. Thomas — Pulmonologist, Kochi

With **₹12+ crore** net worth and accredited investor status, wanted steady income without micromanagement. Added private credit AIFs, REITs/InvITs, retained measured equity, and used selective SIFs for downside control. Predictable cashflows with preserved capital. At scale, structure matters more than returns.

Dr. Ramaiah — Government Doctor, Guntur

With pension support and a conservative mindset, avoided illiquid products and built a balanced equity-hybrid mix supported by a clear SWP plan. Stable post-retirement life without dependency on children. A simple plan followed consistently beats a complex one ignored.

Both prioritised predictability over optimisation.

37.3 — Mistakes, Multi-Asset, and Liquidity

Six mistakes to avoid in the preservation phase:

- Chasing "safe" products with poor real returns
- Locking capital into illiquid schemes
- Exiting equity completely — inflation erodes a debt-only portfolio over 20+ years
- Overloading real estate
- Falling for guaranteed-return pitches
- Delaying succession and estate planning

Multi-asset funds reduce decision fatigue and work well for doctors seeking simplicity — especially when spouses may eventually manage finances. **Liquidity:** maintain 2–3 years of expenses in readily accessible assets. Accessibility matters more than sophistication.

37.4 — Before You Move On

Preservation phase checklist:

1. Equity retained at 40–50% — not exited entirely
2. SWP and income layers designed and running
3. 2–3 years liquidity buffer maintained separately
4. Alternatives capped, exit paths clear
5. Succession, nominations, and will current
6. Portfolio reviewed annually for simplicity and drift

Financial maturity is knowing when protection matters more than progress.

Chapter 38

DISTRIBUTION PHASE CASE STUDIES

Income, Independence & Dignity

38.1 — Performance to Peace

Investing shifts decisively from performance to peace. This phase is not about stopping work — it is about choosing how wealth supports life. Regular income, capital safety, simplicity, and dignity replace return optimisation.

- **Allocation (age 70+)** — 30–35% equity (low-volatility index) | 35–45% hybrid/debt | 10–15% REITs/InvITs | 5–10% cash/liquid buffer
- **Target** — 8–10% XIRR with minimal volatility
- **Priority** — predictable income, capital safety, simplicity, succession clarity, independence from children

38.2 — Four Doctors, Four Distribution Lessons

Dr. Vasantha — Retired Surgeon, Bengaluru

No active income, children settled abroad. Structured income through SWP from conservative hybrid funds, supplemented by REIT distributions and liquid reserves. Stable income without dependence on family. Predictability beats potential at this stage.

Dr. Nalini — Retired Physician, Trichy

Living alone with low risk tolerance. Kept equity minimal, centred portfolio on balanced hybrid and multi-asset funds with a single SWP source. Easy to manage, stable lifestyle continuity. Complex portfolios increase anxiety, not returns.

Same retirement tier. Both built income systems their family could understand and manage independently if needed.

Dr. Abraham — Retired Orthopaedic Surgeon, Mohali

Large corpus and accredited investor status. Reduced alternatives exposure, structured income through SWP and selective private credit, retained equity as inflation hedge. Ensured clear will and PoA documentation. Stable income with smooth succession clarity. Structure matters — even in late life.

Dr. Krishnamurthy — Retired Government Doctor, Vijayawada

Pension income and modest investments. Supplemented cashflow through SWP and REIT income while maintaining a healthy liquidity buffer. Comfortable lifestyle without financial anxiety. A modest but well-planned portfolio is enough.

Same clinical retirement tier. Both proved that simplicity and clarity produce outcomes as durable as complexity.

38.3 — Mistakes and What Protects Against Them

Five mistakes in the distribution phase:

- Chasing higher returns instead of income stability
- Investing in unfamiliar products late in life
- Locking capital into illiquid schemes
- Overly complex portfolios — harder to manage, harder to hand over
- Ignoring succession and estate planning

Multi-asset funds are especially suitable where spouses or family may eventually manage finances. Keep **12–24 months of expenses** instantly accessible.

> **Liquidity is not a return asset — it is a dignity asset.**

38.4 — Before You Move On

Distribution phase checklist:

1. SWP aligned to monthly cashflow needs
2. Equity retained at 30–35% as inflation hedge
3. 12–24 months liquidity buffer instantly accessible
4. Simple, transparent product mix — family can understand it
5. Succession plan, will, and nominations current
6. Trusted advisor accessible for annual review

True wealth succeeds when it supports life — without dominating it.

Chapter 39

The Doctor's 40-Year Wealth Blueprint

Learning • Earning • Teaching • Giving

39.1 — A Blueprint, Not a Prediction

Doctors understand long-term protocols in medicine — yet investing often becomes reactive. Wealth is built not by responding to short-term noise, but by executing a disciplined plan consistently over decades. **A blueprint provides structure, not prediction.**

39.2 — The Four Decades of a Doctor's Life

An eminent orthopaedic surgeon once described a doctor's life in four decades: *Learning · Earning · Teaching · Giving*

It is not merely a professional sequence. It is a life philosophy. Every doctor lives these decades. Few prepare for their transitions. When wealth is structured with intention, it allows each phase to unfold with clarity, stability, and dignity.

39.3 — Decade 1: Learning — Accumulation

The decade of sacrifice and time advantage. Small, disciplined investing builds familiarity with markets and establishes behavioural strength early. Compounding rewards time — not income size.

You do not need to look wealthy in your 20s. You need to think wealthy.

39.4 — Decade 2: Earning — Growth

The acceleration phase. Income rises, responsibilities expand, allocation discipline becomes critical. Avoiding large allocation mistakes matters more than chasing exceptional returns.

This decade decides whether money becomes your servant — or your master.

39.5 — Decade 3: Teaching — Preservation

Professional maturity peaks. Wealth shifts from acceleration to continuity. Stability, liquidity, and structured income take precedence. The objective is not maximum return — it is continuity.

39.6 — Decade 4: Giving — Distribution

Simplicity and predictability. Systematic withdrawals, reduced volatility, succession clarity. Distribution must be deliberate — not improvised. *Liquidity, in this decade, preserves dignity.*

39.7 — Asset Allocation Across the 40-Year Journey

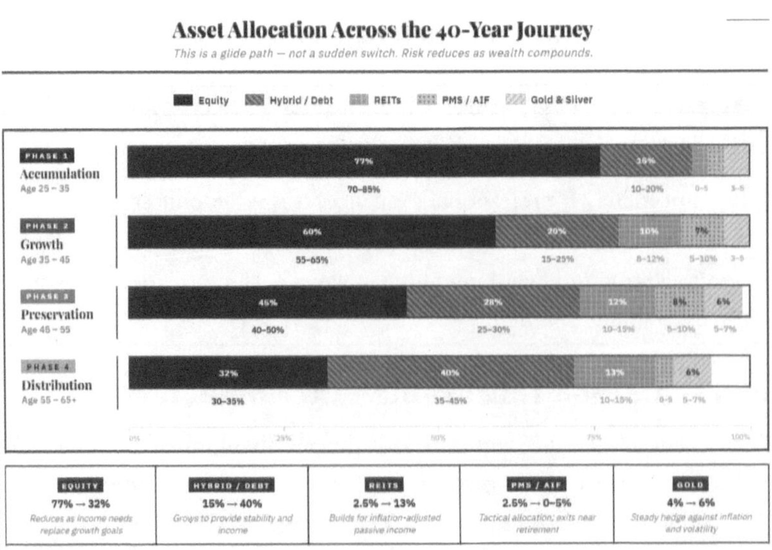

Figure 39.7 — Each phase flows naturally into the next.

39.8 — Where Doctors Commonly Deviate

- Over-allocating to real estate at every phase
- Parking excess cash in low-yield FDs
- Reacting to short-term market noise
- Investing without exit clarity
- Ignoring liquidity needs

Deviation creates friction. Discipline creates momentum.

39.9 — The Right Advisor, India's Runway, and Periodic Review

The right advisor aligns wealth with life stages, manages behavioural risk, optimises post-tax XIRR, and ensures disciplined rebalancing. The structural edge often exceeds advisory fees many times over.

India's growth story — demographics, rising incomes, deepening capital markets — makes this blueprint especially powerful here. See Chapter 6. Global exposure adds diversification; India remains the core compounding engine.

Stress-test every 2–3 years: income shifts, risk tolerance changes, evolving goals, liquidity needs. Blueprints evolve. Principles don't.

39.10 — The Blueprint in One Thought

Most doctors move naturally from Learning to Earning. Few move deliberately into Teaching and Giving.

Why? Because wealth was not structured early enough.

Freedom at 60 is engineered at 35.

Learning builds awareness.
Earning builds scale.
Teaching requires stability.

Giving requires freedom.

Strategic wealth creation allows all four to unfold with intention. Not just money. *A life aligned.*

Chapter 40

The One-Page Financial Plan for Doctors

40.1 — Why Doctors Need a One-Page Plan

Doctors handle complexity daily, yet the most effective medical protocols are simple, structured, and repeatable — *your financial life deserves the same discipline.* A one-page plan cuts through noise and prevents costly mistakes during market stress.

If your financial plan cannot fit on one page, it is too complex to follow.

40.2 — What This One Page Represents

This page is not a product list, a return promise, or a static document. It is a **decision framework** — a behavioural anchor and filter for new ideas across life stages. Doctors who follow a one-page plan rarely panic, overcommit to illiquid assets, or chase financial fads.

Simplicity enables discipline. Discipline enables outcomes.

40.3 — The Doctor's One-Page Financial Framework

A. Purpose & Goals

- **Target financial independence age: ________________**
- **Monthly post-retirement income needed (₹):____________**
- **Major goals (education, clinic, legacy): ______________**

B. Asset Allocation Glide Path

Accumulation → Growth → Preservation → Distribution. Full glide path with percentage bands — *see Chapter 39, Table 39.7.*

C. Investment Rules (Non-Negotiable)

- Liquidity before lock-in
- Exit clarity before entry
- Regulated products only
- Real estate exposure capped at 25–30% of net worth
- Alternatives ≤15% of net worth
- Gold only for diversification — ETFs and multi-asset funds preferred

D. Behavioural Guardrails

- No tip-based or "guaranteed return" investing
- No large cheques without a cooling-off period
- No panic selling during market falls
- No concentration in a single asset
- No March-only tax investing

Behaviour protects returns more than intelligence.

E. Insurance & Safety Net

- Adequate term + health insurance with super top-up
- Emergency fund: 2–3 years of expenses
- Professional indemnity insurance

F. Retirement & Income Strategy

- Self-created pension via market-linked instruments
- SWP-based income model
- Hybrid and REIT income layers
- Equity retained for inflation protection
- No forced annuities

G. Succession & Continuity

- Will in place and registered
- Updated nominations on all accounts and policies
- Power of Attorney executed
- Asset and document list maintained and reviewed annually

H. Review Rhythm

- Annual portfolio review
- Rebalancing on allocation drift
- Life-event-based adjustments
- Advisor consultation for major changes

40.4 — How Doctors Should Use This Page

Print it, keep it visible, and store it digitally. Revisit it before major investments, during volatility, when income shifts, or when peer influence creeps in. If an idea violates this page, reject it. If it aligns, evaluate it calmly.

This page is your filter, not your to-do list.

40.5 — Why This Page Works Over Decades

This framework adapts without drifting, grows without greed, and protects without fear. Doctors who follow a clear structure make fewer decisions — but consistently better ones. *In investing, consistency beats intensity.*

40.6 — Final Words to Doctors

You do not need to master finance — you need a clear structure, a trusted advisor, and the discipline to stay the course. Wealth is not about proving intelligence; it is about enabling freedom, dignity, and choice.

Treat your finances the way you treat your patients: *with care, patience, evidence, and long-term thinking.*

Glossary

Strategic Wealth Creation for Doctors

Investing in India's Compounding Decade

Key terms and concepts used throughout this book, arranged alphabetically. Where an acronym is in common use, it is listed under the acronym with the full form shown below it in italics.

A	
AIF *Alternative Investment Fund*	SEBI-regulated pooled investments in assets like private equity, real estate, and structured strategies, typically for high-net-worth investors.
Alpha	Return generated above the benchmark. Reflects investment skill, not market movement.
Asset Allocation	Distribution of investments across equity, debt, real estate, gold, and cash. It determines risk and long-term returns.
Asset Concentration Risk	Risk from excessive allocation to a single asset class, reducing diversification and liquidity.

B	
Behavioural Bias	Emotional or psychological tendencies that lead to poor financial decisions, such as fear, overconfidence, or herd behaviour.

C	
Capital Appreciation	Increase in investment value over time.
Cash Flow	Movement of money into and out of personal or professional finances.
Category II AIF	Funds investing in assets like real estate and private companies for long-term growth, without leverage.`
Category III AIF	Funds using advanced strategies including derivatives and long–short investing to enhance returns.
Compounding	Process where investment returns generate additional returns over time. The primary driver of wealth creation.
Corpus	Total accumulated investment value.

D	
Debt	Fixed-income investments such as bonds, debt funds, and fixed deposits, offering stability with moderate returns.
Diversification	Spreading investments across assets to reduce risk.

E	
Emergency Fund	Liquid savings set aside to cover unexpected expenses or income disruption.
Equity	Ownership in businesses through shares or equity mutual funds, offering high long-term growth potential.

F	
FD *Fixed Deposit*	Bank investment offering fixed returns over a defined period, often failing to beat inflation after tax.
Financial Independence	Stage where investments generate enough income to cover living expenses without active work.

H	
Hybrid Fund	Mutual fund investing in both equity and debt to balance growth and stability.

I	
Illiquidity	Difficulty in converting an investment into cash quickly without loss.
Inflation	Increase in prices over time, reducing purchasing power.
InvIT *Infrastructure Investment Trust*	Investment vehicle providing income from infrastructure assets like roads and power projects.
Investment Ratio	Percentage of income invested regularly.

L	
Lifestyle Inflation	Increase in spending as income rises, reducing investment capacity.
Liquidity	Ease of converting investments into cash quickly and efficiently.

M	
Mutual Fund	Professionally managed pooled investment vehicle investing in diversified assets.

N	
Net Worth	Total assets minus total liabilities. True measure of financial position.
Nominal Return	Investment return before adjusting for inflation.

O	
Opportunity Cost	Potential gain lost by choosing a lower-return investment.

P	
PMS *Portfolio Management Service*	Professional management of customised investment portfolios.
Portfolio	Total collection of investments owned.

R	
Real Return	Return after adjusting for inflation. Reflects actual wealth creation.
REIT *Real Estate Investment Trust*	Investment vehicle providing income from commercial real estate without owning physical property.
Retirement Corpus	Total accumulated investment used to generate retirement income.
Risk	Possibility of loss or lower-than-expected returns.

S	
Safe Withdrawal Rate (SWR)	Percentage of retirement corpus that can be withdrawn annually without exhausting funds, typically 3–4%.
Sequence Risk	Risk of poor returns occurring early when withdrawals are being made.

SIF *Specialised Investment Fund*	SEBI-regulated investment vehicle combining features of mutual funds and alternative investments.
SIP *Systematic Investment Plan*	Regular fixed investment into mutual funds to enable disciplined investing and compounding.
STP *Systematic Transfer Plan*	Gradual transfer of money from one investment to another, typically debt to equity.
SWP *Systematic Withdrawal Plan*	Facility allowing periodic withdrawal from investments.

T	
T+1 / T+2 Liquidity	Settlement time after selling investments. T+1: money received in 1 working day. T+2: money received in 2 working days.
Tax Efficiency	Structuring investments to maximise post-tax returns.
Term Insurance	Pure life insurance providing financial protection without investment component.

V	
Volatility	Short-term fluctuations in investment value.

W	
Wealth Creation	Process of building financial assets through disciplined investing and compounding.

X	
XIRR *Extended Internal Rate of Return*	Actual annual return accounting for timing of investments, withdrawals, and cash flows.

Note: *Tax rates, regulatory thresholds, and product parameters cited in this glossary reflect provisions current at the time of writing and are subject to change. Verify current rates with your Chartered Accountant or SEBI-registered investment advisor before making financial decisions.*

Appendix A

Assumptions Used in Illustrations

The numerical illustrations in this book are based on reasonable long-term assumptions drawn from historical Indian market data and prevailing financial conditions. These assumptions are used solely to explain concepts and demonstrate the impact of compounding, inflation, taxation, and liquidity.

Where required, the following broad assumptions have been used:

Asset Class / Parameter	Assumed Return Range
Equity	12–14% per annum
Debt	6–8% per annum
Hybrid / Balanced strategies	8–11% per annum
Real estate	5–8% per annum
Inflation (general)	6–7% per annum
Lifestyle inflation for doctors	8–12% per annum

Actual returns vary across time periods and investment choices. The purpose of these illustrations is not to predict future performance, but to highlight structural relationships between return, time, inflation, taxation, and investor behaviour.

Appendix A forms part of Strategic Wealth Creation for Doctors and should be read alongside the main text.

Appendix B

Methodology and Return Measurement

This book emphasises real return, liquidity, and sustainability of wealth, rather than nominal return alone.

Return Measurement Framework

Where investment performance comparisons are shown, the Extended Internal Rate of Return (XIRR) framework has been used wherever relevant. XIRR accounts for the timing of cash flows, duration of holding, and sequence of investments and withdrawals, and provides a more accurate representation of actual investor experience than simple averages or CAGR.

Case Illustrations

The case illustrations presented in this book are based on real-life behavioural patterns and financial situations observed over years of the author's professional interactions with doctors. Names and identifying details have been changed to protect privacy.

Objective

The objective throughout the book is to focus on decision quality, allocation discipline, and long-term compounding behaviour, rather than any individual outcome.

These illustrations are intended to represent common financial patterns observed in the medical profession.

Appendix B forms part of Strategic Wealth Creation for Doctors and should be read alongside the main text.

Appendix C

Disclaimer

This book is intended solely for educational and informational purposes. It does not constitute investment advice, financial advice, tax advice, or a recommendation to buy or sell any specific investment product, security, or strategy.

All investments involve risk, including the possible loss of capital. Past performance does not guarantee future results. Readers should evaluate their own financial situation, risk tolerance, and investment objectives carefully.

Before making any financial decision, readers are strongly advised to consult a SEBI-registered investment advisor, Chartered Accountant, or other qualified professional.

The author and publisher shall not be held responsible for any financial decisions taken by readers based on the contents of this book.

Regulatory frameworks, taxation, and investment rules are subject to change over time.

Appendix C forms part of Strategic Wealth Creation for Doctors and should be read alongside the main text.

Appendix D

How to Use this Book

This book is designed as a practical framework, not a one-time read. The chapters are arranged in a logical sequence. The early chapters focus on identifying structural gaps, behavioural patterns, and common financial traps faced by doctors. The later chapters explain asset allocation, liquidity management, and long-term wealth structuring.

Readers will benefit most by approaching the book in three stages:

- **Stage One — Build Awareness.** Identify which situations, habits, and patterns described in the book apply to your own financial life.
- **Stage Two — Build Structure.** Use the frameworks discussed to improve liquidity, investment allocation, and financial stability gradually over time.
- **Stage Three — Build Consistency.** Wealth creation does not depend on individual investment decisions alone, but on sustained discipline and continuity.

Financial independence is not created by reacting to markets, but by following a clear, structured approach over many years.

Readers are encouraged to revisit relevant sections periodically as their career, income, and financial responsibilities evolve.

Where required, readers may seek professional guidance to implement these frameworks in a structured manner.

Appendix D forms part of Strategic Wealth Creation for Doctors and should be read alongside the main text.

Connect with the Author

Tejaswi Sanga

CMT | CFTe | Financial Strategist & Wealth Advisor

tejaswi@compoundrx.in

For queries on wealth strategy and financial planning for doctors:

Scan to visit my website

Scan to chat with me on WhatsApp

www.ingramcontent.com/pod-product-compliance
Lightning Source LLC
LaVergne TN
LVHW090317210926
848480LV00001B/274